YOU ARE NOT WHAT YOU WEIGH

YOU ARE NOT WHAT YOU WEIGH

escaping the lie
and living the truth

lisa bevere

CREATION HOUSE
Orlando, FL

Scripture quotations marked RHM are from
The Emphasized Bible: A New Translation by Joseph
Bryant Rotherhan, copyright © 1959, 1994. Used by
permission of Kregel Publications, Grand Rapids, MI.

Interior design and typography: Lillian L. McAnally

LIBRARY OF CONGRESS CATALOGING-IN-PUBLICATION DATA

Bevere, Lisa.
   You are not what you weigh / Lisa Bevere.
   p. cm.
ISBN 0-88419-542-2
1. Overweight women—Psychology. 2. Body image
in women. 3. Obesity—Psychological aspects. 4.
Obesity—Religious aspects—Christianity. 5. Body
image disturbance. 6. Self-esteem in women. I.
Title.
   BF697.5.B63 B48 1998   98-41550
   248.8'43—ddc21   CIP

89012345 BVG 87654321

Printed in the United States of America

Every year over a thousand women die senseless, hopeless deaths. They die trying to win approval that will never be granted. These are determined and strong women with wills of iron. Yet their very wills are used against them and honed into weapons of self-destruction. Perhaps you know someone with an eating disorder. Perhaps even now she is holding this book.

This book is dedicated to every woman who has ever struggled with her physical image. It is penned to each of you who found yourself encumbered and entangled inwardly to your outward physical self. This is a book of truth to dispel the lies that have held you captive for far too long. It is a sword placed in your hand to cut the tethers and ties that bind you. I have fought on this battleground and won. I will be a true friend and share with you the Truth that set me free.

ACKNOWLEDGMENTS

To my husband, John—you have never reduced me to what you saw or what I weighed, and I love you for it. I am so blessed to have a husband like you to support me and remind me of God's unconditional love for me. You are my best friend.

To my four precious sons—Addison, Austin, Alexander, and Arden—thanks for all your help. I love you all more than words can say. May you always know true beauty. Stay strong and free!

To Tina—you are one of the most beautiful women I know.

To the staff of JBM—Mike, Amaryllis, Tarah, and Chris—thanks for the babysitting and back rubs.

With deep appreciation to Tom Freiling and the entire Creation House staff—you encouraged me to dig deeper into this subject. Your support and encouragement have meant a lot.

To my heavenly Father—Your Son has been the truth that set me free. You delivered me from a dungeon of sin and darkness and set my feet on the pathway of light. Forever I will praise Your name.

Contents

THIS BOOK IS NOT
ABOUT INFORMATION;
YOU'VE HAD ENOUGH OF THAT.
IT'S ABOUT TRANSFORMATION.

INTRODUCTION

W HY WOULD I FEEL DRAWN TO WRITE A BOOK on the subject of weight? Because I have experienced both ends of the spectrum: I've been overly thin, and I've been overweight. I remember and can keenly identify with the frustration and pain of those who suffer from eating disorders. I will share an in-depth account of my struggle. But first I need to introduce myself.

I do not come to you as an expert on diet, nutrition, or exercise. I'm sure you have already amassed enough knowledge in these three areas. Nor do I address you from the vantage point of an aerobics instructor, beauty queen, or critic. I'm sure you have had encounters with all of these. I come just as a friend.

I fought this battle alone. It was my secret struggle for years. I waged a silent inner war, afraid to tell others... afraid they might mock me if they knew. I never realized how many others wrestled with the same fears and failures until I had already come out on the other side.

If only there had been someone in my life with whom I could identify, one who not only understood but had waged her own battle—and won—it would have been easier for me. But there was no one.

It was never a lack of knowledge that held me bound. I knew the caloric count of practically everything I ate. I also knew the amount of calories each aerobic and anaerobic exercise burned. I pored over health manuals and periodicals; I took classes and purchased magazines, devouring any information that promised me a new body by summer or in time for the Christmas holidays.

I was afraid. I didn't believe I could succeed, so why should anyone else believe in me? I imagined I was surrounded by people who expected failure from me. Though I know now my assessment was not true, I believed it nonetheless. All the while, I was my own worst critic and believed in my *self* the least of all. There seemed to be two of me—one I protected, the other I projected. I protected my *self* not out of love, but out of fear. *What if everyone knew the truth?*

I pretended to be confident when actually I was afraid. I pretended to be angry when actually I was hurt. I pretended to be strong when actually I was weak. I projected an image I thought would be accepted because I was certain *the real me* would be rejected. I decided it was okay if people rejected the fake me, but not the real me. She would remain hidden.

Over the years I have learned something about images or facades. They use up entirely too much energy in their maintenance, leaving us drained and void of the power to change or develop the real. Soon we are confused about who we really are. Stepping out from behind these illusions leaves us vulnerable, but there is no reason to fear, for we will only be vulnerable with each other and, of course, with God.

God will not hurt you, and so I cannot. Through these pages you hear my words, in private and in the tone and time of your own choosing. I am not there to argue with you or to criticize you. I am only there to support you and lead you to Him.

I promise to be open, honest, and transparent with you. I can willingly share my failures because He has turned them into triumphs. If you identify with the messenger, you are more receptive to the message. On these pages I will share with you the Word of God, which has become flesh in my life because it alone bears the seed of incorruptible power to produce and affect any lasting change or healing in yours.

This is not a book about *information;* you already have that. It is about *transformation.* May its message transform you by the power of the Holy Spirit.

—Lisa Bevere
Orlando, Florida

TYRANNY CREATES A BONDAGE
SO FAR-REACHING THAT
ITS TENTACLES ARE FELT
IN EVERY AREA OF LIFE.

THE TYRANNY
OF THE LIE

GOD IS COMMITTED TO FREEING HIS CHILDREN from every present lie, snare, and bondage. *Tyranny* is a very strong word, one that describes an actual stronghold. It describes a process of thinking so oppressive and hopeless that those under its domain soon become depressed and disillusioned. Those under tyranny are held captive beneath the heavy weight of constant failure, pressure, and accusation. Tyranny creates a bondage so far-reaching that its tentacles are felt in every area of life.

Webster's Dictionary defines a *tyrant* as

"one with a tyrannical or compulsive influence." A tyrant can never be pleased. No effort presented by his subjects is ever quite good enough. A tyrant will not grant any lasting approval to those in his vice grip, for tyranny gains its power through constant *disapproval* and *abuse* of its subjects. Those under its power labor tirelessly under the false hope that one day they will please their master and be rewarded. Then they will be whole, happy, free, and loved.

But this is a lie. This taskmaster will not be pleased; he refuses to be. He is always manufacturing yet another image of perfection with which to taunt his subjects—one that is younger, stronger, thinner, and more beautiful. Though you know you can never match this image, you continually strive for acceptance.

There is a way of escape. If you're imprisoned, you can be free. If you know someone who is a prisoner, they too can escape. There is a route that transports us far beyond the reach of a cruel and harsh taskmaster, a path that leads to freedom. Perhaps you've tried and failed. Maybe you're discouraged and frustrated, or you've just had enough. Possibly someone you care very much about is currently held captive. *Now* is the time to walk away from it all.

STOP!

I want to radically interrupt your torment. I believe you can be free from the bondage of weight—whether you're anorexic, bulimic, or overweight. Your present outward condition reflects a deeper inner turmoil. This captivity did not start on your exterior frame. It began in secret, deep within, and it has worked its destruction *from the inside out*.

It could have been last year, five years ago, or a very long time ago when these deep-seated lies were whispered into the inner recesses of your mind. At first you thought the voice was a friend. So you listened. "You could look that good if you just lost ten pounds!" "Exercise, and you'll look better."

Then the voice intensified its attack: "Don't eat that; it will make you *fat!*" "She *is* thinner than you!" "Look! Your stomach is sticking out."

Then, "You're huge!" "You're disgusting!"

At first its helpful hints help keep you in check. Then come the comparisons. Then the whispered accusations progress into a critical, nagging obsession. Soon you are not only listening—*you're believing*. Deception spreads from the realm of your thought life and spills out until it weaves itself into the very fibers of your physical body. It even distorts the visual perception of your eyes until all you see in the mirror is failure. It continues its constant conversation of correction and comparison in your mind. The voice harasses and accuses you daily. Its hold is so strong it is almost...*spiritual*.

Before we go further I want you to answer some questions honestly. Don't give the answers you think sound right; there is no one grading this, and you will only cheat yourself if you are not 100 percent honest. As you listen for answers you may hear two voices with conflicting opinions. So listen with your heart, not your head; it will not lie to you.

Did you recognize this voice I have just described? _____

_____

How loud is it? Do you hear it even when others are talking to you? _____

_____

_____

How often does it interrupt your thoughts: monthly, weekly, daily, hourly, or more often? _____

_____

What does it say to you? _____

_____

Are these the words and descriptions of a
friend? _____

_____

Do you believe them? _____

Can you silence the voice? _____

I want to share a truth with you: It is not
meant to frighten you, but *what holds you
captive physically is rooted in the spiritual*. It
has grown from a seed, a word, a disap-
proving glance, a rejection, a comparison. It
was planted deep into the soil of a wound in
your soul during a time (or many times) when
rejection or acceptance of you as a person
was based on your physical form. Or perhaps
it was planted during a time when your
person was violated in such a painful way
that you decided to barricade your *self* physically from the world rather than endure that
kind of pain again. Or perhaps you just
bowed under the weight of the constant barrage of negative, accusing messages sent by
our cultural advertising and negligent entertainment media.

How can one resist and overcome such
influences? How can wounds so deep and
secret ever be healed? You must first *know
who you really are*. As a human, you are created in the image of God, and there are
multiple dimensions of you.

> Then God said, "Let us make man in our image, in our likeness..." So God created man in his own image, in the image of God he created him; male and female he created them.
>
> —Genesis 1:26–27

First, there is the physical or natural dimension of you. It is what you see when you look in the mirror. It is the image reflected and projected to others. It functions in conjunction with the five senses. It sees, smells, tastes, hears, and touches. It is the outer shell that houses you. It protects, nourishes, grows, reproduces, ages, and eventually dies.

This physical realm can be broken, scarred, wounded, healed, and strengthened. To some degree it can be altered, but physically each of us is the product of a genetic compilation passed down through centuries of reproduction. Our physical bodies are not unlike fruit trees, which grow from seed form to full maturity. We pass through stages of growth and harvest, each varying in their timing and season.

Our physical body in itself is a testament to the glory of God. In all of man's years of study it is still a mystery. Man cannot create; he can only clone, or re-create, human life. We cannot *produce* life; we merely *reproduce*. A creator originates, not duplicates. God is the *Creator* of all life. He is the Creator of your individual life and physical form. He was intimately involved in each and every detail. Surely you have witnessed the miracle and wonder of a baby. It is the very handiwork of God.

> You knit me together in my mother's womb. I praise you because I am fearfully and wonderfully made; your works are wonderful, I know that full well.
> —PSALM 139:13–14

We can all look at a baby and see the miracle, but can you look at your *self* today and say the same? Can you call your *self* fearfully and wonderfully made? Or is the wonder crowded out by a list of shortcomings and flaws? Don't answer me; I already know your answer.

Your physical *self,* though the most obvious, is the least representative of the real you. The physical can only touch physically. You cannot physically reach within your *self* and touch your soul. *That* is the real you.

Though you cannot touch it and though you've never seen it, you know your soul is there. The soul has a range of emotional senses all its own. It is the part of you that *feels*—not physically but emotionally. In your soul you experience happiness, sadness, joy, and pain. If you were ever made fun of, it was your soul—not your physical body—that experienced the pain.

The soul consists of your mind, will, and emotions. It is the place of expression of your person—your *personality*. It houses your thoughts, your hopes, your dreams, your fears. Though the physical cannot reach in and physically touch the soul, your soul is nourished by physical affection as well as wounded by physical abuse. A hug can spill over from the physical and warm your soul. A slap can sting your heart as well as your face. Your soul lives in your body. It can *exercise power* over your physical body.

In times of danger, the soul can override the body's physical capacity. We have all heard stories of great feats of strength where will has overcome matter, where the human desire is so great it supersedes physical odds. This can be found with athletes or with a parent whose child is in danger. There are also accounts of those who have been paralyzed by fear—physically capable yet frozen by sheer will power.

The soul can imprint itself on us outwardly. Fear, grief, or anger can etch themselves upon a face after years of expressing physically the inner turmoil of the soul. Likewise, joy, peace, and strength can leave their mark on a face. Fear of rejection can change a person's posture, causing one to cower or stoop, while confidence holds another erect and straight.

Just as our physical bodies were created by God, so is the soul.

> For you created my inmost being…
> —PSALM 139:13

The soul is the inner being. It should be governed by the will, which is governed by our strongest base of influence. It draws information from our mind and considers our physical needs in its analysis of natural information. It draws on past experiences and is forged and molded with each passing day. It can be both analytical and emotional. The soul is different from the physical body, yet the soul inhabits the body much as a hand fills a glove. The body is lifeless, expressionless, and useless without the soul.

A third dimension is the spirit, which is often described as your *heart*.

> Love the Lord your God with all your heart and with all your soul and with all your mind and with all your strength.
> —MARK 12:30

This scripture lists these different avenues of expression in order of their preeminence:

1. Our heart or spirit
2. Our soul
3. Our mind and strength

When our lives are divinely ordered, our spirit will direct our soul and mind, which in turn will guide our physical self. It is the goal of this book to introduce truths to you that will lead you into a proper restoration of all of these areas. If you are ready for transformation, "then you will know the truth, and the truth will set you free" (John 8:32).

Let's pray together at the close of this chapter and ask God for truth and discernment.

Father,

In the name of Jesus, I ask that Your truth would light the paths of my inner heart, that I might hear the still, small voice amid the din of any other influence or opinion. Lord, You fashioned and formed me in the secret place of my mother's womb, not for bondage but for liberty. Though I cannot go back to the quiet stillness of the womb, I now ask You to fashion me once again, in the secret place of my heart. Create a place of refuge and peace where there has been turmoil and torment. It is safe to be honest with You, for You could never hurt me. You have already proven this by dying for me so I might live. With You I will be honest, for I know You are the Truth that sets me free. Amen.

Personal Notes

WE NEED TO KNOW TRUTH
WITH A DEEPER INTIMACY
AND TO A GREATER DEGREE
THAN WE'VE KNOWN THE
LIE . . . FOR ONLY TRUTH STOPS
THE PROGRESSION OF LIES.

2

THE TRUTH

I N THE LAST CHAPTER WE CLOSED WITH A DISCUS-
sion of truth—or more specifically, *the Truth*.
We need a frame of reference for this truth. It
cannot vary, and it must be much higher and
far greater than any truth our culture or med-
ical science has already offered. To obtain this
level of truth, we must move beyond the
mere opinions of mankind. We need to
pursue truth that is formative and able to re-
create, able to bring healing and restoration,
and able to carry within itself a seed of life.

It must supersede the authority of any other

present truth or fleeting cultural trend. These vary and fluctuate with the whims of media and men. It must never change, and thus it must be timeless. It must be truth that is ancient, because it existed *before* us and will continue on long *after* us. It must be eternal truth.

Eternal truth cannot be found within the confines or reasoning power of mortal man. The created cannot create. We can be creative; we can reproduce. But we cannot *initiate creation*. No man is supreme in authority. Even if an individual or government could rise to such a level, it would only be for a moment, a tiny speck on the timeline of eternity. No man lives forever.

This eternal truth must be born out of a motive so pure no human could conceive it. It must come from someone superior to humans in every way. It can only come from God:

> "My thoughts are completely different from yours," says the LORD. "And my ways are far beyond anything you could imagine. For just as the heavens are higher than the earth, so are my ways higher than your ways and my thoughts higher than your thoughts."
> —ISAIAH 55:8–9, NLT

God is making it very clear: He doesn't think like us. Because we are merely the created, we cannot even *imagine,* or image in our mind,

14

His ways. So expansive is this gap that He uses something we can see—the distance spanning the heights of heaven and the terrain of earth—to describe it. Can a man standing on this earth reach up and touch the heights of heaven?

No, even from Mount Everest—earth's highest mountain—this is impossible. There is a great expanse between the way we think, reason, dream, hope, and live and the way God does things. As a matter of fact, He doesn't *do* things—He *embodies* them. We live; He *is* life. We love; He *is* love. We think; He *is* knowledge, wisdom, and understanding. We dream; He *is* the fulfillment of every dream, even ones we are not yet capable of conceiving.

These comparisons are made to explain that from where we are, we can never apprehend or comprehend His thoughts or ways. Being earthbound, we are bound to time; we think and live relative to time. He is boundless because He lives in the realm of the timeless eternal. We all had a beginning and, most likely, an end. He has no beginning; He *is* the beginning. He always was…always will be.

This alone is a hard concept for us to grasp because everything we have ever known or experienced had an origin, a beginning. We can grasp the concept of having no end, but having no beginning is a hard concept to comprehend. Though change and new beginnings are fathomable to our human mind, no beginning and changeless are not.

Though one nation may conquer and dominate another, elevating one leader above others for a short time, the winds of change will blow. Yet God is the Ruler Supreme over all the nations, the King over every earthly king or kingdom. He outranks any natural or spiritual authority and power. He is the *ultimate authority*.

Every created thing—all creation—is under the authority of God. Therefore, we can safely say that His voice or opinion overrides all others. The cumulative wisdom of all mankind is foolishness to Him.

> For the wisdom of this world is foolishness in God's sight. As it is written: "He catches the wise in their craftiness"; and again, "The Lord knows that the thoughts of the wise are futile."
> —1 Corinthians 3:19–20

Again, this is a contrast between the entire world's cumulative wisdom and God's. He declares the thoughts of men useless or futile. The entirety of the world's wisdom is hopeless.

It is only His truth and wisdom that bring hope, fruit, and lasting liberty. Man may *know* truth, but God *is* truth.

> Then you will know the truth, and the truth will set you free.
> —John 8:32

16

To *know* truth is to be intimately acquainted with it. Knowing is more than the mere acknowledgment of its existence. It implies a relationship. *Strong's Exhaustive Concordance* defines the term *know* as found in this scripture as "absolutely; in a great variety of applications and implications; an adherence to truth not only on a mental level thus changing our perceptions on merely a single level, but one which permeates until it reaches every area of our being."[1] This is what happens when truth becomes a part of us.

We need to know truth with a deeper intimacy and to a greater degree than we've known the lie. We once lived a lie, and it captivated us. If we live the truth, it will liberate us. To *know* truth is to *live* truth. It is the truth we live that sets us free. Then it penetrates deeper and reaches further than the lie, dispelling with its light any darkness lurking in the remote areas of our soul. Knowledge of the truth alone will not be enough. We need a *relationship* with truth. The question changes from "*What* is the truth?" to "*Who* is the Truth?"

I am married, and though others may know about my husband or know him personally on some levels, they will never know him in the same way or dimension I do. They may be acquainted with John Bevere the friend, minister, author, employer, or father. But I alone know him on the intimate, private level of *husband*. That is *our* relationship. Though others may know him by what he does, I know John Bevere by who he is. We are one.

We must become one with the truth because we have been one with the lie. Who is the Truth?

> Jesus answered, "I am the way and the truth and the life."
>
> —John 14:6

He is the way we seek. He is the Truth who sets us free. He offers each of us the life we long for. You may right now be questioning what I say: "I know Him, but I do not feel free. I feel captive!" He allows captivity to serve as an invitation to experience Him on a deeper level. He is drawing you closer, drawing you deeper, to His side. He wants to be your companion and Lord as you journey from captivity to freedom. He does not want you to try it in your own strength again. You've already tried and failed.

He wants the glory from this escape. All He requires from you is a deeper level of surrender to truth, a yielding of your will to His. Before you travel further, you must prepare an atmosphere for transformation.

Jesus,

I have known You as Savior, Teacher, and Lord. I ask You to reveal Yourself to me as the Truth. Let this light pierce through the dark-

*ness of the lie. You are the Word made flesh.
As I submit to Your Word, let it become flesh
to me. I embrace You and Your Word as the
final and ultimate authority in my life.
Unveil my eyes that I might see You and in so
doing I behold the Truth. In Your name.
Amen.*

It is important to realize something: Lies are
more often easier to embrace than truths. One
lie is easily followed by another and yet
another until the truth is found out. *Only
truth stops the progression of lies.* When we
are constantly bombarded with lies, we begin
to believe the lie. Likewise, when we lie to
others or to our *selves* long enough, we are
soon deceived and begin to believe the lie
and doubt the truth.

*Transforming truths are usually the most
costly to embrace.*

God offers these truths to whosoever will.
Though they cost the very life of His Son, He
freely and generously calls to all who have an
ear to hear:

> Come, all you who are thirsty,
>   come to the waters;
> and you who have no money,
>   come, buy and eat!
> Come, buy wine and milk
>   without money and without cost.
> —Isaiah 55:1

This would seem to be a contradiction of what I said earlier. I said the truth was costly—yet God says it is free. Transforming truth is costly because it requires an admission of our own inability to provide. It is a call to lay aside our pride and surrender to humility and dependence. God continues:

> Why spend money on what is not bread,
>   and your labor on what does not satisfy?
> Listen, listen to me, and eat what is good,
>   and your soul will delight in the richest
>   of fare.
> Give ear and come to me;
>   hear me, that your soul may live.
> I will make an everlasting covenant with
>   you,
>   my faithful love promised to David.
>   —Isaiah 55:2–3

God questions them: "Why do you spend your money, your time, your *self,* on that which will never satisfy you? Your thirst is not quenched, your hunger is not abated, your achievements are empty." When we have spent our *selves* of our natural strength, resources, talents, and provisions, God invites us to come to Him empty-handed. He does not want our money or labor—He wants our empty lives. In exchange for our surrender, He gives us life, an everlasting covenant, and faithful, unwavering love.

But we cannot come to Him in the strength of our own merits. We must strip our *selves* from the lies and embrace His truth. He is calling us to the river of baptism, where we are totally immersed into life, and all that is death is washed away. Such a rebirth is available for every area of our lives.

We must acknowledge our need for Him, our need for His help. We must ask Him to sow a seed of truth into the soil of our humbled heart. This seed is found in His Word.

> As the rain and the snow
> come down from heaven,
> and do not return to it
> without watering the earth
> and making it bud and flourish,
> so that it yields seed for the sower and
> bread for the eater,
> so is my word that goes out from my
> mouth:
> It will not return to me empty,
> but will accomplish what I desire
> and achieve the purpose for which I
> sent it.
>
> —ISAIAH 55:10–11

The seed of truth is first planted in the rich soil of your spirit. Guarded there, it is allowed a safe atmosphere in which to grow. As it grows, we must tend it as we would a natural garden, watering it with the truth of God's

Word and uprooting any additional weeds of destruction and deception.

Everything God does in our lives begins in seed form. This is an eternal pattern:

> As long as the earth endures, seedtime and harvest, cold and heat, summer and winter, day and night will never cease.
> —Genesis 8:22

Seeds are planted; they grow until harvest; then the entire cycle repeats. Seeds represent not only natural plants—they represent every living thing in God's creation. Every living thing carries the seed of regeneration. Even words and deeds can be seeds.

Some of the seeds that have been planted in your life may have been seeds that produced pain or destruction. Such seeds need to be uprooted. New seeds of truth should be planted—ones that will yield a harvest of healing and strength for your life.

Cold and heat represent the two extremes of conditions facing all seeds or plants. Summer and winter represent the two most diverse seasons of weather. Day and night, dark and light, are the daily cycle of renewal.

If the earth is still present (which of course it is!), then these cycles and seasons of change and harvest are continuous in your life. Your physical body is subject to these same conditions. This is a new day, a new season for you. A time to plant new seed and reap a harvest of fresh produce in your life. I know you are ready for change.

This will mean uprooting old plantings and reconditioning the soil to create an atmosphere for the new. God is the ultimate gardener. He takes the soil of a fearful, hardened heart, breaks apart the weeds of fear and hardness, and plants new seeds, turning that heart into a garden of strength, joy, and life.

Are you ready to allow the Master Gardener to transform you? If so, pray this prayer:

Heavenly Father,

You said that I could come to You with nothing but my failures, and You would give me water that would quench this thirsting in my soul. You invited me to dine on the Bread of Life and to partake of milk and wine. I have tried to satisfy my self with bread, and it failed me. I have tried to comfort my self with milk and console my self with wine, and they failed me.

Yet You speak of water, bread, wine, and milk I cannot provide. It is only found in You. Forgive me for my foolish efforts to satisfy my self with natural food. It does not fill me; it only postpones temporarily my real longing—which is for You. Lord, let me be as the woman at the well; give me living water. I humble my self and confess my need and utter dependence on You in the area of eating.

Lead me in Your paths, and I will walk in them. I don't want to walk alone in this area any longer, I invite You into this area in my life. Transform it! In Jesus' name. Amen.

Have you ever trusted someone, only to be disappointed by that person? _____

_____

_____

Have you ever disappointed your self? _____

_____

Have you ever really believed or thought something to be true, only to find out later that it was not? _____

_____

Have you ever lied to others? _____

_____

Have you ever deceived your self? _____

_____

Personal Notes

_____

_____

_____

_____

_____

_____

_____

_____

_____

_____

_____

_____

_____

_____

_____

_____

_____

**THE GOAL OF A FALLEN
CULTURE IS SEXUAL
DESIRABILITY OR
ATTRACTIVENESS.**

3

THE IMAGE OF THE LIE

IF JESUS IS THE EXPRESS IMAGE OF THE TRUTH, then what is the express image of the lie? Just as truth needs an image for expression, power, and validation, so the lie must have an image, or it remains powerless.

Actually, we are made painfully and constantly aware of this image of the lie. It is everywhere we even happen to glance. It is projected on television and at the movies, on billboards, and splashed across magazine covers and assorted catalogs. Most of us encounter it daily on one level or another. It is the image built by multitudes of advertising and media experts who feed off our cultural external influences. It is the image of this present culture's ideal woman. In her *self,* she is nothing; it is what she *represents* that endangers us.

There are multiple portrayals of her. She is presented to all ethnic groups. She is a woman, perfectly at ease with her *self.* She moves freely in any setting. She is adored by men and envied by women. All other women are harshly and unfavorably compared with this nameless woman. She never ages; behind her facade of perfection she mocks and makes note of every flaw and imperfection of others.

Her skin is flawless in tone and complexion. Her nose is straight—not too small or too large. Her eyes are bright and lack any dark shadows, circles, or lines around them. They are encased in luminous, wrinkle-free skin. Her lips are full and artfully shaped. Her teeth are perfect and gleaming white. Her hair is whatever ours is not.

Her body is perfectly proportioned and sits atop long, strong legs. Her breasts never age (or nurse)! All too often they are not even real. She is either taller or shorter than us— the perfect height!

This image is never what we are and is always just beyond our reach, taunting us with her seductive eyes. Who is she anyway?

Her name doesn't really matter; she is not

real. She is an image molded and forged by
the spirit of this world. What she doesn't
have, plastic surgery readily supplies. Even
this computer generation will not tolerate any
imperfection in her—it reduces her thighs and
cinches her waist while sweeping away any
sign of imperfection in her skin. She is a deaf,
dumb, and blind idol.

Though we know she is not real, young
girls and older women look at her in awe.
The young are inspired, and the older are
depressed.

Why would someone we have never met
be able to influence us so profoundly?
Because we have not allowed the imprint of
God to influence us as deeply as she has
influenced us. Without a definitive raising of
His standard, we have accepted the seductive,
graven image of the world.

> The fashioners of an image—all of them
> are emptiness, and the things they
> delight in cannot profit.
> —Isaiah 44:9, RHM

To *fashion* something is to make, model,
form, or manufacture. In the Bible the words
image and *idol* are used interchangeably with
the exception of two references. Therefore
we could go into the above scripture and
bring it forward into today's terms. Then it
would read:

> The fashioned idol, modeled idol, or
> fashion image—all of them are empty
> and lifeless. What they value and prize
> *cannot* profit or help you.
>
> —Author paraphrase

Isaiah tells us in the second part of this
verse why this is so: "For their idols neither
see nor know. No wonder those who worship
them are so ashamed" (TLB). The ancient idols
or graven images were forged by craftsmen
who made them out of wood or stone.
Sometimes they were overlaid with precious
metals or costly jewels. But they were never
more than lifeless—dead—wood or stone. No
matter how dressed up they were on the out-
side, they had no life on the inside.

The people would model and form images
and idols and then bow down to what they
themselves had crafted. These crafted images
(of wood, stone, or precious metals) were
made by the created (humans). Then the created subjected themselves to the crafted.
Crying out to images without breath, those
with eyes asked guidance of blind idols.
Those with breath, mouth, and voice cried
out to mute idols with lifeless lips. Those with
ears to hear cried out to deaf ears of stone.
They offered fragrant incense and food to
idols who could neither smell nor taste.

The created longed to worship the work of
their own hands, though these idols could

never raise a finger in response. The created cannot *create*—it can only *craft*. The crafted cannot even craft.

It all seems rather silly to us. Most of us would never bow our knees to an idol or seek wisdom from a graven image. So what does this have to do with us?

When we worship the works of our hands or the works of the flesh, we are worshiping images of the *creation* and not the *Creator*. Let's go into the New Testament to find how this could be relevant today:

> For although they knew God, they neither glorified him as God nor gave thanks to him, but their thinking became futile and their foolish hearts were darkened.
>
> —ROMANS 1:21

They knew there was a Creator God, but they did not want to glorify Him or acknowledge His provision by thanking Him. They turned their eyes from God and began to worship images. Soon their hearts became like the idols they worshiped—void of light and futile. This parallels Isaiah's description of useless idols.

The image you behold is the image you become—not outwardly but inwardly.

The concept is further expanded by Paul the Apostle in the Book of Romans:

> Although they claimed to be wise, they
> became fools and exchanged the glory
> of the immortal God for images made to
> look like mortal man and birds and ani-
> mals and reptiles.
> —ROMANS 1:22–23

The idol worshipers claimed to be wise cre-
ators, but when you bow to that which is
equal (mere man) or lower than your *self,* you
become degraded, abased, and deceived.
When you serve what is lifeless you die.

> Therefore God gave them over in the
> sinful desires of their hearts to sexual
> impurity for the degrading of their bodies
> with one another. *They exchanged the
> truth of God for a lie,* and worshiped
> and served created things rather than
> the Creator—who is forever praised.
> Amen.
> —ROMANS 1:24–25, EMPHASIS ADDED

They wanted to serve the works of their
flesh, so God let them become mastered by
their flesh. They worshiped images fashioned
after their own desires, so God turned them
over to their basest of desires. Where there is
idol or image worship, we always find sexual
sin. It comes in the form of promiscuity and
perversion. Sexual impurity is accompanied
by an increased prominence of sexual expres-

sion. Nudity is common. What once was saved for intimacy is now displayed for all to view. Men and women who were inwardly fashioned for the habitation of the Spirit of God instead become temples of sexual perversion and depravity.

Sexual suggestion is used to sell everything in our current culture. The goal of a fallen culture is sexual desirability or attractiveness. You can study any fallen ancient culture and find this to be true. In today's culture, those who are not viewed as sexually desirable are not assigned much worth. The undesirables are the older, the overweight, and the out of shape.

If you are afraid of being sexually abused, you will often hide your *self* within walls of excess flesh or starve your *self* in an attempt to return to your childhood. To our culture, sexual perversion or promiscuity is merely physical. Unfortunately, this physical-body mentality has even crept into the church. Yet we know there is a much deeper and stronger spiritual connection tying the physical/sexual realm to the unseen spiritual/worship realm.

We exchange the truth for a lie whenever we worship or serve the created and not the Creator.

Before we go further it is important to describe the worship of idols or idolatry in contemporary terms. For until we do so, idolatry still may seem a foreign term. *An idol is anything you draw your strength from or give your strength to.* It is how you spend your *self*—your time, your efforts, your thoughts. It is the driving force behind your actions. It is what makes you feel confident and comfortable. *Nelson's Illustrated Bible Dictionary* defines an *idol* as "something we ourselves make into a god."[1] It can be anything that stands between us and God—a substitute for God.

As Christians it is important to determine whether we are serving an image of God or God Himself. There are three options:

❧ Unwittingly we may fashion or mold our own image to serve.

❧ We may bow to the one our culture readily provides.

❧ We may cry out to God and ask Him to reveal Himself (and in response, we worship Him).

Our image of God is an image that will service our *selves*. It is the god of *me*. It is the result of trying to conform God to our image. He may be a hard taskmaster or a "sugar daddy," based on our unique and individual frame of reference. But this image or idol is a mere spectre of the real. It is limited to our own past experiences and perceptions. It is forged in the realm of our reasoning, and we have already learned that God sees things completely differently than we do (Isa. 55:8–9).

If we are serving the gods or idols of this world, we will recognize this in our desire to conform to the world's image. We will want the acceptance and approval of our culture. We will desire what our culture desires. We will seek its reward and system of social and financial security. The image will always be before us, inviting and enticing us to be like it. We will look toward it, gauging our success or failures according to the messages we receive from these idols.

If we are serving God and not merely an image from any other source, we will experience a constant and ongoing transformation into His image. *All lasting liberation, healing, or change begins with inward transformation.*

If we are truthful, we will admit to visiting all three temples: the god of flesh, the god of soul, and the God of spirit.

There are multitudes of books offering outward information—diet plans, exercise regimens, self-improvement suggestions for your makeup or wardrobe. This book is not one of those. Whatever God does in your life, this will last. The time is short, and this message is urgent. *God is calling us to radical transformation.*

You've known the lie; you've been introduced to the truth. Now it is time to be honest. What image are *you* serving?

Have you cried out to fashioned idols and images? _____

_____

Did you long to be conformed to their shape, size, or image? _____

_____

Did you think they would bring you love and happiness? _____

_____

Did they answer your prayers? _____

Have you confused being seductive with being beautiful? _____

_____

Have you traded sexual desirability for purity?

_____

Are you ready to repent of admiring the idols and images of the world? _____

_____

Have you served a god in the image you have made? _____

_____

Have you thought that transformation would be much too difficult for God to accomplish in your life, so you've continued to struggle in your own strength? _____

_____

_____

Are you ready to repent of reducing the image of God to your own level of understanding, reasoning, knowledge, ability, or experience? _____

_____

Are you ready to renounce the hold of man's religion and embrace God on His terms? ___

_____

By repenting, you renounce the hold and influence of the idols in your life. This will be an act of submission to God and aggression against a long-term spiritual stronghold in our culture. Please feel free to mix your own words with the words of prayer printed on this page.

Father,

I come before You in the name of Jesus, in the name of truth. Lord, I repent of looking to the graven images and idols of this world when I should have come to You for my strength. I renounce their hold and influence in my life. I cast their impressions from my mind and their illusions from before my eyes. Father, remove the veil from my eyes. I want to see You and You alone. Let Your image outshine any other in my life. Imprint Your truth deeper within me than any of the lies of the false god of this age. I turn from the image of the lie toward the knowledge of Your Son. Reveal Yourself to me in a deeper and very real way. I give You permission to invade this private and personal area of my life. In Jesus' name. Amen.

Personal Notes

_____

_____

_____

_____

_____

_____

_____

_____

_____

_____

_____

_____

_____

_____

_____

_____

_____

_____

SELF IMAGE IS
A DEFENSIVE MECHANISM.
IT IS THE IMAGE WE PROJECT
WHILE WE TRY TO PROTECT
WHO WE REALLY ARE.

4

THE IMAGE
OF SELF

In the last chapter we introduced the image,
or idol, of the lie. There is yet another area of
"image worship" that needs to be confronted
in our process to freedom. We have been
imprisoned by deceptive lords—ones who
tricked us into allegiance and then threw us
into dungeons and prisons when we didn't
meet their incessant demands. Through
repentance we are removed out from under
their legal jurisdiction and freed to live under
the authority and protection promised in the
kingdom of God.

> He has rescued us from the dominion
> of darkness and brought us into the
> kingdom of the Son he loves.
> —Colossians 1:13

All forms of captivity are under the authority and dominion of darkness. By renouncing our allegiance to their cause and wholeheartedly asking the Lord to forgive any sympathy or inclination toward their domain, the power of His Son is there to rescue us from the images that have held us captive. Having renounced any tendency toward the image of the world, it is now time to go a step further and renounce another prevalent image.

This image is much more subtle and widely accepted in most religious circles, though it is not found on any list in the kingdom. It actually is a religious idea, one of the very first to be introduced. Yet, there is a problem with religious ideas and traditions; they are powerless to liberate us. Jesus explained it this way:

> You have let go of the commands of
> God and are holding on to the tradi-
> tions of men...setting aside the
> commands of God in order to observe
> your own traditions!...Thus you nullify
> the word of God by your tradition that
> you have handed down.
> —Mark 7:8–9, 13

It is yet another example of turning away from the living commands of God to conform to the wisdom and traditions of man—an example of turning from the Creator toward the created. Jesus explained that in so doing, they nullified—negated or canceled out—the very power they needed. Power is not found in principles but hidden within the Word of God. The religious people of Jesus' day exchanged the truth for a lie, life for death, and power for impotence.

We need the Word of God, for hidden in its manifold truths is the *power* of God. Though the word of man may contain form and structure, without the life and power of God it is useless. It cannot transform our hearts though it may please our heads. We need substance and relationship. To apprehend this we must strip away yet another veil, the veil of *self worship*.

You may immediately reject this, arguing, "How could I worship my *self?* I feel bad about my *self*. I have a bad *self* image!"

To this objection I would counter, "Whenever you are limited to your *self* image, then the *image of self* becomes your master."

At this time I want to challenge some typical deceptions. Here is one: *If only I could feel good about my* self, *then I would be fulfilled.*

God does not want us fulfilled through the avenue of *self*. He wants us fulfilled through

Him. The Word of God is not set up to cause us to feel *good* about our *selves*. It is set up to reveal to us a *good God*. To *feel* good about our *selves*, we have to *be* good. But even Jesus would not assign the adjective of *good* to Himself.

> "Why do you call me good?" Jesus answered. "No one is good—except God alone."
> —Mark 10:18; cf. Luke 18:19

Notice He did not say, "Wow, God must have told you that! Thanks, I really feel encouraged and much better about My *self*. I am good, and you can be good, too! Just follow Me!"

No, His answer to the rich young ruler was of a very different sort. He wasn't looking to be labeled as "good" by human standards; His goal was to glorify His heavenly Father, who is the very essence of goodness.

Though Jesus was the Son of God, He did not grasp at equality with God the Father by calling Himself good. God alone is good, and through His goodness we are restored, and He is glorified.

I want to address *self* image on two levels: first, on a personal level and secondly, on a spiritual level. An image of *self* is not something we are born with; it is forged through pain, pressure, and praise.

Pain will cause us to become aware of something of which we previously were not aware. When I had my first son, the delivery left me with back problems. Until then I never even noticed my back. Now, pain brought it to the forefront.

Pressure will bring hidden or under-the-surface talents or flaws to the surface. Competition is set up with pressures to pit one against another in a setting where the talents and abilities of one will contrast with the others. A child might think he is the fastest runner in his class, but until race day it is not known.

Praise will test what you are made of and point out talents or assets. The Bible tells us a person is tested by the praise he receives (Prov. 27:21). One of my children received a lot of attention for his hair. It was something he couldn't care less about, but it constantly set him apart when he received comments like: "Your children are handsome—especially this one. Look at his hair!" Being a boy, these comments bothered him, and we eventually cut his hair. But a girl might have been tempted to draw her *self* worth from such compliments.

These processes cause us to become aware or conscious of our *selves,* or *self* conscious. A collective number of common occurrences raise our level of awareness of what was previously not apparent to us.

For example, my three-year-old son is beautiful, yet he is totally unaware of the concept of beauty. This unawareness makes him that much more attractive. His goal is not to be attractive, but to be expressive. His objective is to give love and receive love. He doesn't even know the color of his eyes. However, he knows he is loved, cared for, and to whom he belongs—and those things are enough for him. He is free!

I see it in the pictures he draws and hear it in the animated tone of his voice. He likes to hold my face between his two soft hands and look at me face to face. He wants me up close in order to know he has my full attention and affection. He looks me intently in the eyes until I return his gaze; then he kisses me. He needs the closeness. In it, he is not aware of his *self*—he is only aware of the two of us.

This is what God wants for us—that we might be so totally aware of our relationship with Him that we lose consciousness of what is around us. He doesn't want to draw us close to see our flaws; He wants to hold us close to captivate us with His love.

Recently I had a vivid dream in which the Lord spoke passionately to me in that twilight before waking: "Don't just glance at Me; I want you to behold Me. I want you held captive by My gaze."

I realized He was asking for a new level of intensity in our relationship. I saw my *self* glance over to Him for guidance, direction, or protection—looking, then turning away, looking, then turning back to what was in front of me. When I heard His call to behold Him, my gaze became fixed upon Him.

When John and I were first engaged, we could be in a room full of other women and men and yet only see each other. If I left the room, I'd return to find him watching for me. His eyes would light up when he saw me. Our eyes would lock and that would be it. Unless we were interrupted, no one else existed for us. I wasn't aware of my *self;* I was only aware of *us.* It was no longer "John and Lisa"; it was an awareness that the two of us were one.

Each of us began life with this same unawareness of self, but when did it leave? I believe this usually happens progressively as we are exposed to the opinions of others and when we allow those opinions to influence us more than the opinions of God.

Somewhere between childhood and adulthood we lose our bearings. Whether we intended to or not, we exchanged the truth for a lie. We began to believe we are what we do, what we have, what we wear, what we know, how we look, who we know, and *what we weigh*.

I remember acutely being thrust into this arena of *self* consciousness, very much against my own will. When I was five years old, I lost my right eye to cancer. This meant going to school with a patch over my eye until the swelling went down and the eye socket was ready to be fitted with a prosthesis. I remember beginning kindergarten as a normal child and two weeks later returning as a freak. I was intensely aware of the stares and jests of my peers. It was more obvious than the gauze adhesive bandage on my face. The bandage no longer seemed to cover merely my eye. Now my very soul felt entangled and entrapped in that gauze bandage.

I no longer felt free of my *self*. I felt restrained by it. I began to scan the faces of others to see how I should feel about my *self*. If they were repulsed, then it meant I must be repulsive. I didn't question their assessment. My first-grade picture shows a very different girl from the one found in my kindergarten photo taken before my eye was removed. There had been more than an eye loss; there had also been a loss of innocence. I had lost a great measure of my *self* unawareness, and with it I had lost my confidence. Before I lost my eye, my confidence was not placed in how I looked. I had been unaware of my looks. I had been free. Now I was bound to my looks as surely as a prisoner bound by chains.

For each of us it happens in different measures and at various times. Whenever there is diversity or differences, we find comparisons and criticism. Most of us remember the agony we all endured during puberty at various times and stages. That's when I remember being most body conscious. I felt as though my body had betrayed me.

I was a very late bloomer, and I decided I didn't want to bloom at all. I came to this conclusion after hearing from my peers who had gone before me, and from watching various health movies, what I would have to endure. I did not want bra straps for boys to snap. I had no desire to shave my legs and underarms. The very thought of bleeding and cramping monthly sounded like a horrible intrusion on my favorite sport—swimming. (Twenty-five years later it still does.)

Each girl was assessed according to her physical development. Boys noticed the girls who were developing quickly. Gone were the days of equal chest size. For me the word *flat* took on a totally new meaning. I learned the art of creative draping during PE class as I tried to maintain a delicate balance between getting in and out of my gym suit and my clothes. I was beginning to feel a further separation between the *physical* me and the *real* me...the *obvious* and the *unseen*.

As children, our bodies served us, but it was not long before we found our *selves* serving them. Perhaps you were an early bloomer. You were made aware of your physical side in a positive light. But still you were reduced to something temporal and subject to change. People praised the obvious while missing the unseen. So you developed the obvious and neglected the unseen.

Self image is a defense mechanism. It is the image we project while we try to protect who we really are. It's the projected image versus the protected one. *Self* image is the one left vulnerable when we lose the innocence of *self* unawareness. In a moment's time, most of us lose the unconscious sense of our physical body. In that instant we became tethered to what has now become awkward and uncomfortable.

The opposite of *self* conscious is not a "good" *self* image or *self* esteem. The opposite of *conscious* is *unconscious*. To lose consciousness of one's *self* happens when we become more conscious or aware of *God* and His will than we are of *self* and its will. This is a work of the Spirit, accomplished progressively as we renounce our natural limitations and abandon our *selves* to Him.

What incident (positive or negative) of being tethered to or measured by your physical self comes first to your mind?

_____

_____

How old were you? _____

Describe your *self* before this incident—how you looked at your body and how you felt.

_____

_____

_____

_____

Describe your immediate reaction to this incident, if you remember it.

_____

_____

_____

_____

In what areas are you still *self* conscious?

_____

_____

_____

_____

Would you like to be untied from these images, whether they are good or bad? To no longer be limited to *self's* perception?

_____

_____

_____

Let's pray and sever those ties:

Dear Father,

I want to be free like a child again. Untie me from self and bind me to You. I don't want to be alone and aware of me; I long to be aware of us. I turn my eyes from the image of self and direct them toward Your face. Draw me close that I might behold You and be held by You. I tear down the idol of self and build the altar of God. In Jesus' name. Amen.

PERSONAL NOTES

_____

_____

_____

_____

_____

_____

_____

_____

_____

_____

_____

_____

_____

_____

_____

_____

TURNING FROM THE TRUTH
TO A LIE CAUSES US TO LOSE
SIGHT OF THE ETERNAL
AND BECOME LIMITED
TO THE OBVIOUS.

5

THE ROOT
OF IMAGE

In the last chapter we discussed the personal, or soulish, root of *self* image or consciousness; now I want to dig deeper and go down to the very origin of *self*. Where did this consciousness all begin? We find the first awareness or awakening to *self* in Genesis, the book of beginnings:

> The man and his wife were *both naked*,
> and they felt *no shame*.
> —Genesis 2:25, emphasis added

Adam and Eve were both *naked* and *un-ashamed*. They were undressed and unaware of their nakedness. They were conscious only of the perfect union that existed between them—separate, yet one; individual, yet complementary; different, yet similar. It was an awareness so intense and complete that it overshadowed their physical *selves*.

Their interaction was not limited to the physical realm . . . that would come later. They responded to their oneness, their union. They celebrated their mutual uniqueness, their complementary differences, and the attributes that distinguished them from every other creature in creation.

The Bible offers no description of their stature, skin, or hair coloring. It is unimportant. It doesn't even give their ages at this introduction. We have no idea whether Adam and Eve were thin or fat, tall or short, black or white. I am sure they embodied and exemplified pure physical perfection—the perfection of the origin of the species of human life in a time before disease, sickness, and death.

Shame had yet to creep between them. It did not exist in this garden of creation. Not only were they naked before each other, both were completely uncovered in the presence of their Creator. Free in His presence and in the presence of each other. God and Adam rejoiced freely in the glorious dawn of God's last living creation: woman.

This innocent beginning was conceived in a perfect environment, an atmosphere of perfect unity with each other and their Creator. Their awareness encompassed three areas: the Creator; the creation that flourished, sheltered, and provided for them; and one another. We cannot be sure how long this time of innocence endured.

But all too soon their innocence was lost forever. They were made aware of their *selves*. With their awareness of *self* came an awareness of their distinct inequality with God. And thus they were about to be tempted with the knowledge of good:

> "You will not surely die," the serpent said to the woman. "For God knows that when you eat of it *your eyes will be opened,* and you will be like God, knowing good and evil."
> —GENESIS 3:4–5, EMPHASIS ADDED

They were presented with the ultimate temptation, the ultimate perfection—*to be like God*. To have your eyes opened to the way things really are...to pass from the dependency of children and know good from evil without any involvement of authority...to be lord of your *self*. It was an appealing proposition. The serpent promised them an opening of their eyes, implying they were blinded to some part of the big picture. Could something they needed have been obscured from their present level of vision?

They'd never known or experienced *evil*. It is also quite possible that they hadn't even known *good*. *They'd only known God.*

> And the Lord God commanded the man, "You are free to eat from any tree in the garden; but you must not eat from the tree of the knowledge of good and evil, for when you eat of it you will surely die."
>
> —Genesis 2:16–17

The knowledge of good and evil is the law of sin and death. God wanted Adam to remain free in the liberty of his knowledge of God. Adam had gained this knowledge, or relationship, by walking with God. His relationship with God was not based on rules—it was grounded in love. Adam did not need the knowledge of good and evil to walk with God—he already walked with Him. Satan did not want Adam and Eve to remain free and alive under the law of liberty, so he perverted God's warning of protection.

They listened to his lie and exchanged their pure knowledge of God for the knowledge of good and evil. In that moment their thoughts and ways became completely different from His. God never serves His *self;* He is Father in the purest and truest sense of the word.

Adam and Eve had experienced God on an intensively intimate and pure level. He'd formed them lovingly with His hand and quickened them with His very breath. In foolish rebellion they turned from the Creator and chose to embrace the created.

> When the woman saw that the fruit of the tree was good for food and pleasing to the eye, and also desirable for gaining wisdom, she took some and ate it. She also gave some to her husband, who was with her, and he ate it.
> —GENESIS 3:6

The fruit of the forbidden tree looked good and pleasant. It could impart wisdom. This sounds like our description of an idol, doesn't it? As Eve reached for the *fruit* of creation, she turned her back on the *God* of creation. As Adam took the fruit from the hand of his wife, he dropped the hand that forged him.

> Then the *eyes of both of them were opened,* and they realized they were naked.
> —GENESIS 3:7, EMPHASIS ADDED

Adam's and Eve's eyes were opened; for the first time they perceived their nakedness. The Bible does not say that their clothes fell off and then they realized they were naked; it says that their *eyes were opened*. The veil or covering had not been around their *bodies*—it had been over their eyes.

Now they saw into a dimension previously shrouded from their view. Stripped of the eternal veil of light, they beheld the dark and earthly dimension. A veil of light had cloaked their eyes. It was replaced by one that draped their hearts. This shrouding of the heart created a habitation for darkness.

The Book of Romans tells us: "Although they claimed to be wise, they became fools" (Rom. 1:22). Only a fool exchanges truth for a lie...the unseen for the seen...the temporal for the eternal.

Their transgression was accompanied by a heightened consciousness of *self*. Sin gave birth to shame. Innocence and purity were replaced with knowledge and sensuality. This new sight required a veiling of their bodies.

> ...so they sewed fig leaves together
> and made coverings for themselves.
>   —Genesis 3:7

Sin always requires a covering. Sin opened their eyes to the visible and closed them to the invisible. They gained sight of reality and lost sight of eternity. Fear dimmed their new sight, for the light within had turned to darkness.

Thousands of years later, Jesus described the mystery of the relationship between the eyes and the soul with these words:

> The eye is the lamp of the body. If your eyes are good, your whole body will be full of light. But if your eyes are bad, your whole body will be full of darkness. If then the light within you is darkness, how great is that darkness!
>
> —MATTHEW 6:22–23

Before their transgression, their eyes had been good and their beings flooded with light. They had seen only light. In the presence of God there is only light—there was no shadow about Him. Light dispels darkness. There was no shame, for shame requires shadows. But living now in the temporal, they knew both good and evil. Now their eyes beheld darkness. There was no light within— only darkness.

Yet, in their fear they retreated into deeper darkness in the shadows of the trees. Darkness will always flee from the presence of light.

> Then the man and his wife heard the sound of the LORD God as he was walking in the garden in the cool of the day, and they hid from the LORD God among the trees of the garden.
>
> —GENESIS 3:8

The darkness brought with it fear and foolishness. They thought they could hide from God. They did not want their deeds to be brought to the light, so they withdrew into the shadows of creation instead of falling at the feet of their Creator. The Book of John explains their act of withdrawal into further darkness:

> Everyone who does evil hates the light, and will not come into the light for fear that his deeds will be exposed. But whoever lives by the truth comes into the light, so that it may be seen plainly that what he has done has been done through God.
>
> —John 3:20–21

Adam and Eve had grasped at equality with God. They tried to be like God apart from God. If you believe lies, you become afraid of truth. Turning from truth to a lie causes the light in us to become darkness. We lose sight of the eternal and become limited to the obvious. *Self* lives in the realm of the seen, the obvious, and the earthly. The consciousness of *self* is a direct result of the Fall.

It is imperative that these truths are fixed and established in your life. Eternal truths produce eternal results; temporal, or temporary truths, produce temporary results. To eradicate a lie you must go back to the truths that existed before the lie.

I find it amazing there is no physical description of Adam or Eve. Their appearance and age are not an issue. We do not find physical descriptions of any individuals until after Adam and Eve have left the garden.

Only then were men and women defined by age, children, labor, and accomplishments. Occasionally we find a person described in terms of his relationship with God. But these are isolated instances and always set apart from the rest. The lives of such people are highlighted uniquely in the unfolding plan of God for mankind.

Sarai, or Sarah, is the first individual to whom a physical description is assigned. Abraham feared the godless culture that surrounded him and his family. Afraid these evil men would kill him and take his wife, he asks Sarai to lie in order to protect him:

> As he was about to enter Egypt, he said to his wife Sarai, "I know what a beautiful woman you are. When the Egyptians see you, they will say, 'This is his wife.' Then they will kill me but will let you live. Say you are my sister, so that I will be treated well for your sake and my life will be spared because of you."
>
> —Genesis 12:11–13

Interspersed throughout the rest of the Old Testament, we find physical descriptions of many leaders: Rebekah, Rachel, Leah, Joseph,

David, Goliath, Absalom, Solomon, and Elisha—to name a few. In the New Testament we find a description of John the Baptist, describing his clothing and appearance. After the description of John, it would appear that the need for physical descriptions became less important. The emphasis switches from the *outward and natural appearance* to the *hidden and eternal person*. From the obvious to the unseen. Why? Because Jesus came to rescue what had been lost in the garden.

Paul describes it this way:

> Therefore, from now on, we regard no one according to the flesh. Even though we have known Christ according to the flesh, yet now we know Him thus no longer. Therefore, if anyone is in Christ, he is a new creation; old things have passed away; behold, all things have become new.
>
> —2 Corinthians 5:16–17, nkjv

As believers we are to change the way we evaluate or view things. No longer are we to know or understand people according to what we see in the natural dimension of the flesh. Paul uses the transition through which we pass in our maturing knowledge of Jesus to explain this. At one time, Jesus had walked among His disciples and other believers on this earth as the Son of man. But now He is in heaven, and it is impossible to know Him according to natural terms. We now learn of Him by the Spirit, through the Scriptures. He is progressively revealed, not as the Son of man but as the Son of God.

Jesus' disciples had known Him as the natural man; now He was revealed as the eternal. Paul admonished the believers to adopt this same view of each other—to look beyond the earthly and obvious to glimpse the eternal, the "Christ in [us], the hope of glory" (Col. 1:27).

When we turn to Christ, the shroud of death is stripped away; once again we can glimpse the eternal. It is a process involving the retraining of our minds and wills. Instead of serving self, we must now subject and submit self once again to the Creator. *To lose an awareness of self we must gain an awareness of God.*

Can you now see and believe that physical awareness and captivity to self is rooted in the Fall? I am not talking about a total loss of consciousness where you no longer care for your physical self. I am talking about escaping the realm or dimension where self becomes your master.

If you desire to gain a greater awareness of God, then pray this prayer:

Dear Heavenly Father,
  Please forgive any tendency I have toward

the mastery of self. You said that I was to take up my cross, deny my self, and follow You. Lord, for too long I have not denied my self; I have been overwhelmingly conscious of my self. I have lived to protect and provide for my self. Please forgive me. I renounce the fallen nature that would seek to serve self, and I ask You to teach me to serve You. I want to become increasingly conscious of Your will and ways, and less and less conscious of my own will and ways. Restore my sight. Let me glimpse again the eternal and lose sight of the sensual and earthbound. I avert my eyes from my self and turn them toward You. In Jesus' name. Amen.

PERSONAL NOTES

_____

_____

_____

_____

_____

_____

_____

_____

_____

_____

_____

_____

_____

_____

_____

_____

_____

_____

I LOOKED AT THE HEADLESS
REFLECTION AND REALLY
HATED WHAT I SAW.
I NEEDED TO PUNISH IT
AND TAKE IT BACK UNDER
MY CONTROL.

6

THE REORDERING
OF DISORDER

In this chapter, I share the liberation God has brought in my life with my struggles with eating disorders. Even as I revisit and recount this period of my life, it is hard to imagine I once lived under such captivity. It is now a gray, dark, and distant shadow...almost unreal in contrast to the light and freedom Jesus has brought. This same freedom waits for you. Though your condition and circumstances may vary from mine, God's truth remains steadfast and absolute. It is His deepest desire not only to set you free, but also to banish your deepest and darkest fears.

Eating disorders could be compared to rampant disorder in your living environment, for certainly we live in our bodies. The purpose of this book is to reorder this area of your life. To re-create a comfortable environment for you to live within. To restore and reassign value to the precious and to discard the vile. To breathe life, hope, and direction where there has been discouragement, death, and confusion.

Many of you have already come to the realization that you have exchanged truth for a lie in some areas. Now is the time for a practical application of truth. There is nothing more powerful than the shared one-on-one testimony of what God has done in our lives. I cannot be there personally with you, but through the pages of this book I believe you will hear what I have to say in a very deep and personal way.

When something is in disorder, it is out of order. Like a messy room where everything is in a disarray. You can't find anything in the overwhelming chaos. Items of value and significance are tossed aside onto the floor or under the bed while an empty candy wrapper sits atop a dresser as if on display. Dirty laundry is tossed carelessly on a chair or bed as though it were a decorative throw.

When the disorder becomes overwhelming, then you tackle the mess with passion and

zeal, only to find your *self* once again surrounded by disarray in no time at all.

The key to keeping a room in order is not
constantly picking it up; the key is locating
and correcting the source of disorder. Disorder
may occur for various reasons—perhaps
things were not put back in their proper place
or were never assigned a place. Other objects
may have been given a place that was imprac-
tical. A shortage of time can contribute to a
lack of order. Discouragement and depression
bring apathy and despair—all contributions to
disorder. A lack of training, discipline, or guidance can also contribute to disorder. Whatever
the sources, when you are surrounded by disorder you feel overwhelmed and confused.

Conversely, when a room, apartment,
home, office, or desk is put in order, you feel
surrounded by an atmosphere where much
can be accomplished. You feel free, the
clutter is removed, and tight quarters loosen.
You don't feel so cramped. You can finally
find things! Items that were hidden or mis-
placed are retrieved.

Order begets order. To correct disorder you
must first establish order. Order is the force
that opposes disorder. It can become a very
powerful force in our lives. A life in order has
its priorities correctly assigned and establishes
boundaries to protect these priorities.

God has given us this admonishment in His
Word:

> Do not worry about your life, what you
> will eat or drink; or about your body,
> what you will wear. Is not life more
> important than food, and the body
> more important than clothes?
> —MATTHEW 6:25

Worry is rooted in fear. When we worry or
fret about something, we think incessantly
about it. This is disruptive and destructive to
our peace of mind. Notice that Jesus tells us
not to worry about the big stuff: life, food,
drink, and clothing. He goes on to assure us
that these things will be provided by our
heavenly Father—the One who gloriously
clothes the lilies and feeds the sparrows.

Worry is never constructive, and it is always
accompanied by fear and torment. Worry can
become self consuming. We could rephrase
this scripture in Matthew 6 by interchanging
the phrase "think obsessively about" for the
word "worry." It would then read:

> Do not *think obsessively about* your life,
> what you will eat or drink; or about
> your body, what you will wear. Is not
> life more important than food, and the
> body more important than clothes?

If life is more important than food and the
body more important than clothes, then why
are so many young women dying to look

good in their clothes? Sadly, they do not know their life is more important than their appearance. They sacrifice the greater for the lesser. They have meditated on a lie and forsaken the truth. Statistics tell us that more than a thousand women die of anorexia and bulimia each year. This does not factor in the number of overweight women who die from the side effects of abusive fad diets. There are others who survive, yet their metabolisms remain sluggish from years of extreme dieting.

When does it all begin? Each story is different. Some girls perceive an obsession with weight as a normal rite of passage into womanhood—one they are introduced to as they watch their mothers or older sisters try on clothes in dressing rooms and bedrooms. Their innocent eyes and ears drink in every detail as their mothers try on suits, dresses, pants, and bathing suits. Considering her mother to be the most beautiful woman in the world, a little girl reacts with shock as her mother exclaims in horror:

"Oh I look so fat in this!"

"Look at my stomach sticking out!"

"These jeans make my bottom look huge!"

The little girl may even protest, quickly responding by saying, "No, Mom, you look beautiful!"

But this assessment is brushed aside as childish. "You'll understand when you grow up," her mother explains. So she hurries to grow up. And as she grows, the food disorder begins to grow also.

As you seek to reorder the disorder of your life as a result of your struggle with an eating disorder, I pray that the principles God taught me in my own time of reordering will help you to win the victory in the area of your weight also. *You* are not what *you* weigh as surely as I had to learn *I* was not what *I* weighed. This book would be incomplete if I neglected to share my personal struggle. This chapter is a revised and intimate version of one found in my book *The True Measure of a Woman*.

Perhaps you will recognize someone you know and love in my story. Maybe you will even glimpse a reflection of your *self* in my words.

There was a six-year period in my life when weight dominated my thoughts. I want to take you back there with me. My struggle began years before I became a Christian, yet it continued after I'd become one. It was important enough to God to set me free, and it is a very real account of the gospel of my life. It is an area where the Word of God was truly made flesh in my life.

Until I was sixteen years of age, I had little or no awareness of my body weight. I was only weighed at summer camp (to make certain I wasn't losing weight on a diet of camp food) and at physicals to establish a pattern of growth. I perceived any increase in my weight in the same way I viewed any increase in my height—a sign of maturing.

I was small for my age and always very active, swimming competitively nearly year round on one team or another from the time I was five. With this lifestyle I could eat whatever I wanted, whenever I wanted, without a thought about my weight.

During my sophomore year in high school I decided to run hurdles immediately following the swimming season. Although the coach instructed us to stretch before our practices, I didn't feel it was necessary since I had just finished swimming season and was in good condition. What I did not realize at the time was that swimming develops different muscles than track and field. Though my muscles were toned for swimming, they were not prepared for running hurdles.

One day during the first week I sprinted through my practice like a rabbit—and snapped my Achilles' tendon. I had to be on crutches for a while, and I decided not to swim during my junior year in order for my ankle to heal. All sports stopped, but I still ate as though I were in training.

One day as I walked into the house from school, my father stopped me and looked me over disapprovingly.

"Come over here and turn around," he said. "Boy, those jeans are tight! How much do you weigh?"

"One hundred twenty-eight." Frightened, I had volunteered my summer camp weight. The truth was I had no idea what I now weighed.

"There is no way you weigh that! You're at least one hundred thirty-five pounds, and probably one forty!" he challenged. "Go weigh yourself."

I was sure he was wrong, but I wandered into my parents' bathroom and stepped onto the scale. To my disbelief I weighed one hundred thirty-eight pounds!

Ashamed, I reported back to my father. He told me I was much too big. He warned me about how my weight would affect my desirability as a young girl. Who would want to ask me out if I was fat?

I went to my room to look at myself, really inspecting my body for the first time. I struggled to pull off my jeans—obviously they were too tight! I could see the seam lines and, in some places, even the stitches running up and down my legs. The imprints of the waistband and pockets were embedded around my midriff. I stripped down to my bra and underwear and stood on my bed so I could see my body. My view was limited to my shoulders down.

I looked at the headless reflection and really hated what I saw. I needed to punish it and take it back under my control.

"You're gross and fat!" I chided.

I berated my *self* as I grabbed the various parts of my body, all of which appeared grossly out of proportion. I turned around and repeated the ritual on my backside, then childishly bounced off my bed.

I went over to my closet and pulled out my swimming sweats. I felt better immediately in loose clothes. I felt safe and hidden. Now it was time to inspect my closet...what else was too tight? I pulled the clothes out and tried on different items. Each time something was tight, even if it was something I had simply outgrown, I walked over to the mirror and punished my reflection: "You look fat.... You *are* fat!"

That night under the watchful eye of my father, I denied my *self* seconds and dessert. After dinner I pulled on a down coat over my swimming sweats and ran the snowdrifts until I felt as though my lungs would burst from the cold winter air. I was determined to lose the weight and get back to one hundred twenty-eight pounds.

The next day at lunch I cut back again; I ate only a Big Mac and fries instead of my normal Big Mac, fries, cheeseburger, and a Snickers bar. At dinner each night I cut back on my portions, and after dinner I ran. I pored over articles in my mother's magazines that gave information on weight loss and dieting.

In two weeks I had lost ten pounds. Everyone at school noticed. Even some of the upperclassmen complimented my weight loss. I felt powerful. I had conquered my body. I was in charge of my weight. I would never be fat again. I swam again during my senior year, and I grew an inch, reaching five foot seven inches. My weight whittled down to a muscular one hundred twenty-five pounds. It seemed as if my weight problems were far behind me.

I chose a college far from my hometown in Indiana. I wanted to break away from all that was familiar. I wanted to experience the West, so I traveled to the University of Arizona. I went through sorority rush and pledged a house even before school began. Now I had built-in friends.

I couldn't help noticing all my sorority sisters were tan, thin, beautiful, and blond (at least the majority were blond). Suddenly I felt awkward and clumsy among these svelte Barbie look-a-likes in ponytails. As I compared my *self* with my newly acquired California and Arizona sorority sisters, my one-hundred-twenty-five-pound body looked like an Indiana corn-fed heifer next to a race horse. I tried not to draw comparisons, but it was evident everywhere I looked.

At dinner girls thinner than me would complain, "I'm so fat! Look at these thighs!"

I would, and I realized their thighs were smaller than mine. If they were fat, then I was *obese!*

"How much do you weigh?" I asked one girl.

"One hundred fifteen pounds."

"Oh, you're thin. You're not fat!" I protested.

She jumped up from the table and grabbed the back of her thigh. "Look at all this cottage cheese! I *am* fat."

I felt foolish. I could only see the fat because she had grabbed her thigh in a vice grip. I remained silent as I scooted further under the table and prayed that no one would ask my weight. I was ten pounds heavier than her. It never crossed my mind that I was also three inches taller.

That night in the privacy of my dorm room I checked my own thighs. There it was! I had cottage-cheese fat, too! Maybe she had been hinting about my fat so I would lose weight.

I began to swim and run again. I stopped eating the sandwiches at lunch, eating only the salad. I dropped my weight to one hundred twelve. But still I did not feel thin enough.

At every meal we all discussed the caloric count for each item on our plates. The one who knew the most about dieting was the smartest. We ruthlessly confessed and pointed out our flaws to each other: "Look at my stomach; isn't it disgusting!" we'd complain as we lifted our shirts for inspection.

"Well, look at this!" another would counter

as she pinched her young, taut tan legs, looking for a flaw.

My stomach was flat, my thighs were tan and thin, my arms were muscular and trim, but I had a flaw.

My flaw was my face. Each time I looked in the mirror I saw failure. My jaw is square, and no matter how thin I got it still looked wide. I would stare in the mirror, and all I could see was a huge, fat face staring back. I would critically assess my *self* as though I were an enemy. "I'll get rid of these jowls!" I would say as I grabbed my lower cheeks. At one point during my junior year, I was a size one and weighed only one hundred three pounds. Still my face looked fat when I looked in the mirror. It was all I could see. I didn't notice the gauntness or the veins that laced my neck. My focus was so distorted.

I also had another person in my life who reinforced my warped impression. My boyfriend constantly commented about my face, monitoring my weight carefully. At the time I thought he just wanted me to be the best I could be, but the truth is, he did it to control me.

When I went home for Christmas my mother was alarmed by how much weight I had lost. She was so concerned that she took me to the doctor. He assured her I was still within the safety limits for my height, but when my mother left the room, he asked me if I was trying to lose the weight.

"No, it is just too hot to eat," I assured him. This was a partial truth. Arizona was considerably hotter, and heavy foods did sound uncomfortable.

"Well, just make sure you take care of yourself. Maybe you should get up in the middle of the night and eat a steak!" he winked.

I smiled and finished getting dressed, although the very thought of steak revolted me.

That night my Mother made my favorite meal.

"I'm not hungry," I told her when she encouraged me to eat.

"You have to eat!" she insisted.

"I'll eat later with my friends; I'm going to a party tonight," I replied. "We'll get pizza."

"You need something healthy. You've hardly eaten all day!" my mother answered.

She was right. I had hardly eaten. I was afraid that by coming home I would get fat again. I thought everyone was trying to force food on me. *They just don't want me thin,* I thought to myself. *They're against me. They don't want me to succeed.*

My mom tried to enlist my father's support. "Tell her to eat."

"She'll be fine." He looked up from his paper and smiled at me. I knew my new weight had won his approval. At least *he* wouldn't push me to eat!

I went out that night with my new and improved, tan Arizona body. I felt like a different person. I walked and talked like my sorority sisters. I had learned something else from them, too—how to party! I flitted around the party, drawing strength from this new-found attention.

"You look great! I should have asked you to the prom!" one boy exclaimed.

Wow! Was this real, or was it a dream? Boys who had never given me a second glance in high school, were now asking me out. Later that night, as I lay in bed, I determined never to go back to what I had been before.

When I got back to college I realized I had gained some of my weight back. While complaining to a sorority sister about it, she suggested taking water retention pills. I remembered my mother taking them, but I wasn't sure what they were for.

"Isn't that just for before your period?" I asked.

"No!" she assured me. "I take them every Friday morning so I'll be thin by Friday night!"

It sounded too good to be true. "Are you sure they are okay?" I asked.

"Yes, look...they are not even prescription!" She handed me a box of diuretic pills that looked harmless. The front of the box sported a picture of a happy woman in a bikini. I flipped them over and read the ingredients.

"They've got a lot of caffeine."

"Yeah, it is great...caffeine gives you a buzz! Try one."

I put one in my pocket. I'd always been able to lose weight easily before. I'd lose it again. But this time it took longer.

Meals were getting harder for me to resist. In addition to the calorie counts and diet tips, we all shared a love/hate relationship with food. It was our enemy because it made us fat, but we loved it because it tasted so good!

Food began to hold a different place in my life. I thought more and more about food—not just about my weight. I developed a passion for food and for drinking. I loved everything to the extreme. If I drank, I drank to get drunk. If I ate, I ate until I was engorged and uncomfortable. But I still wanted to get attention for my looks, so I exercised to the extreme. In a constant pursuit to burn calories, I never sat still. I would even shake my legs all through classes or during my study time. I ate excessively—or dieted excessively. There was no in-between. I only thought about school when I had a test. Still I retained a B average.

The law of food restriction had aroused an excessive desire in me. The law always enflames the lusts of the flesh and soul. I could starve myself, but once I started eating there was no stopping until physically I could eat no more or the food was gone. It was either feast or famine.

This is a hard lifestyle to maintain, and I enlisted the help of laxatives, then diuretics, in my battle. By my junior year in college, my body was addicted to them. It no longer functioned normally. Coupled with a stomach disorder I already had, I was in constant discomfort. I was afraid of my own body. *What if I couldn't go to the bathroom? What if I got fat?*

I became ill and ran a constant low-grade fever. A rash broke out all over my upper body. Finally I went to the school infirmary. "How long has it been since your last bowel movement?" the doctor asked, looking concerned as she poked my stomach.

"A month. But usually I go once a week," I assured her.

She shook her head in disbelief. "Honey, you should go nearly every day. We are going to have to do some tests on you."

First they X-rayed me. The results showed that my intestines were backed up to my lungs. Immediately they checked me into the hospital under the care of a specialist. It was a nightmare. They gave me a prescription-strength laxative; when that didn't work, they made me drink a tumbler full of castor oil. The cramping was horrible.

Then I was subjected to a series of enemas, then more tests. I was finally diagnosed with irritable bowel syndrome and severe lactose intolerance. The whole ordeal shook me up so much that I stopped taking laxatives and diuretics. But still I was obsessed with my weight.

At dinner I watched one of my sorority sisters eat. She consumed everything on her plate, and then some. She wasn't fat. How did she do it? I never saw her running or exercising. In private I asked her the secret.

"I eat everything I want, then I go into the bathroom and stick my toothbrush handle down my throat. Then I brush my teeth."

She made it sound so easy.

"Can you show me how?" I asked.

"Sure! After dinner tonight, just come and brush your teeth with me."

That night after dinner I followed her pony-tailed form upstairs to our common bathroom. For the first time I noticed a lot of my sorority sisters walking into the stalls with toothbrushes in their hand.

"Just go in and do it," she said.

I hesitated; I hated throwing up. Did I really want to do this? She smiled and shrugged at me as if to say, "Whatever," and slipped into the privacy of her stall. I listened. It didn't really sound like throwing up, more like choking or coughing.

"Did you...?"

"Yes, it is that easy."

I bravely stepped in my stall and knelt down in front of the toilet. Before this moment, I had only knelt when I prayed my childhood bedtime prayers. Now I was kneeling before a toilet. I jumped to my feet.

"I can't do it," I protested.

"Sure you can. I do it all the time." She encouraged me with the voice of a cheerleader. I closed my eyes, pushed the toothbrush handle toward the back of my throat, and gagged.

"It didn't work!"

"Try again."

I gagged again. My eyes began to water. I stood up. *I can't do this,* I thought. *I'll just have to starve myself or think of something else.* The school year was almost over, and I was still thinner than most of the girls back home in Indiana. I'd figure something out that summer.

By now I was hopelessly chained to the disorder of my weight and food obsession. It would take more than my frantic attempts to learn how to reorder this area of my life.

Does any of this sound familiar?

PERSONAL NOTES

‿✧‿

_____

_____

_____

_____

_____

_____

_____

_____

_____

_____

_____

_____

_____

_____

_____

_____

IF YOUR WEIGHT
CONTROLS YOUR MOODS
AND YOUR LIFE, IT'S AN IDOL.
IT IS WHAT YOU DRAW YOUR
STRENGTH FROM AND GIVE
YOUR STRENGTH TO.

7

THE IDOL TUMBLES

THAT SUMMER PROVED TO BE VERY DIFFERENT from all the other summer breaks I'd had. That summer I heard the gospel for the first time, and I became a Christian. It filled a void in me that I had tried to fill with attention from boys. I began to relax. *God loved me just the way I was.* For a time the voice was silent, and I stopped my excessive exercising, dieting, and drinking; I began to look healthy and relaxed again.

Christians may not drink, but they love to eat. Every social event I attended was centered around food! At church picnics we ate; after church we ate. On dates we ate. I now had a new problem—my excessive tendency to drink had transferred to a consumption of food. I felt permission to eat, but I'd never faced my excessive tendencies until now.

Around Christian tables no one talked about calories or the vices of food. Food was a celebration. I celebrated with them, and before long I had put back on most of the weight I had lost.

It was during this time that I met John. At the end of the school year, I got engaged and needed to return home to Indiana to prepare for the wedding. I was a little overweight, but John didn't seem to notice.

By August my weight had floated back up—and it was no longer muscle. I was totally out of shape, and the weight was clinging to my stomach, hips, and thighs. I had only two months before my wedding. I decided to exercise and get back in shape while I was home.

But home was filled with turmoil, and I responded to this turmoil by eating. If I was bored, I would walk over to the refrigerator, I'd open the door, and I'd look in even though I wasn't hungry. I binged or starved myself. My days revolved around weighing myself, eating breakfast, weighing myself, running errands, eating lunch, weighing myself, making phone calls for wedding arrangements, eating dinner, and weighing myself

again. I became more and more discouraged—
and I binged more and more! As I binged I
assured myself it was all right to eat everything I wanted *today,* because *tomorrow* I
would not eat at all! Then I would eat until it
was painful. I would toss restlessly, experi-
encing nightmares in which I ate everything
in the refrigerator. I would wake in a sweat
and reassure myself that I had not! Other nights
I wrestled dark fears so real that I felt as
though I wore them like a weight on my chest.

The next day would come, and although
I'd determine not to eat at all, thoughts of
food consumed my mind. How good whatever I saw would taste. I would open and
close the refrigerator and freezer...just to
look. I would weigh myself first thing in the
morning and again in the afternoon and
evening. Often I had not even lost a pound!
After an entire day of not eating, the needle
on the scale would not budge off the same
weight I'd been for days. Discouraged, I
would binge again.

I tried liquid diets and high protein diets,
but they failed. I missed John. My parents
were separated. All my friends were out of
town. I was alone, and I felt fat and ugly.

Then came the day of reckoning. With only
four weeks left until my wedding, I needed to
rent a slip for my size nine wedding gown. I
brought my dress to the store with me so we
could determine the appropriate slip style and

length. My wedding gown buttoned almost entirely down the back. I stepped into it and pushed the sides together so the saleswoman could button it.

"Honey, something is wrong," she said as she shook her head.

"What do you mean?" I questioned.

"This must not be your gown. There is no way you fit into this dress! The buttons are this far apart!" She showed me the distance with her with her finger and thumb...it spanned three or four inches.

I was certain she was mistaken, "Here, it may be a little tight, but I'll push it in." I sucked my stomach in and pinched my waist with my hands.

"Sweetheart, there has been a terrible mistake; this cannot be your gown. I still can't close it; the buttons will tear off if I try."

I could feel my face flushing with frustration and embarrassment.

"Just get me the slip, and I'll try it on without buttoning the dress," I huffed.

"Okay." She walked out, shaking her head doubtfully.

Surely she was exaggerating! While she was gone, I whirled around, contorting myself in order to see the back of my gown. To my horror she was right. It was impossible even to make the sides meet—let alone button the buttons. I'd outgrown my wedding gown in just the short time since August!

I placed my order hurriedly for the slip, gathered my gown, and raced home. The gown had been a little tight when I bought it. I had been certain I would lose weight at home—not gain it as I had. I never dreamed I would do this! My parents had spent a lot of money on this gown. Now I wondered if I'd ever wear it.

When I arrived home, I ran straight upstairs to my room. After hanging my dress in the closet, I grabbed my Bible and threw myself down on the hard wood floor. I didn't want the comfort of my bed. I wanted the reality of my dilemma to settle in. I cried until I wept, then I wept until I'd spent myself.

"God, how could You allow this to happen? I don't eat all day, and still I can't lose a pound. If I eat only an apple and a yogurt, I gain a pound. I binge and gain two pounds overnight! I'm tired of trying and failing. Why can't I eat like a normal person?"

I thought of my father's and mother's faces when I told them the news of my dress. I felt overwhelmed and very sorry for my *self*. When the crying was over, a quiet settled over me. It was then I heard a still, small voice.

"Lisa, your weight is an idol to you."

An idol! All I could envision was the picture of a golden calf I had seen in a children's illustrated Bible. I remained quiet and listened.

"When you are lonely, you eat. When you are angry, you eat. When you are bored, you eat. When you are depressed, you eat. When you are happy, you eat."

That about covered it. The voice continued: "You do not come to Me. You do not read My Word. You eat because it is easier."

Every time I did try to read my Bible, the spiritual oppression that I felt in our house was so strong I would fall asleep; yet I could watch TV for hours and remain wide awake. The same thing happened when I tried to pray.

The still, small voice continued, "You feel good about your *self* when you are thin and bad about your *self* when you are not. You are not Spirit led; your weight controls your moods and your life. It is an idol to you."

I saw it. It was all true. Weight dominated my thought life and tormented my rest. I had not even shared my faith with friends for fear I'd be rejected because I was overweight. The tears flowed again, but this time they were tears of repentance.

I saw how I'd drawn strength from my weight and not from God. I measured my *self* by the scales. I was worthy of love if I was thin, but I was not worthy if I was fat.

Once again the voice spoke: "If you'll repent, I will heal your metabolism. Do not diet, and do not weigh yourself. Separate yourself and fast for three days on juices and water, and I will rid your body of its cravings. I will teach you how to eat again. Write down the weight you should be, and put it in your Bible."

I no longer had any idea what my weight should be. I weighed more than one hundred thirty pounds at the time. My mind flashed with figures from the many weight charts I'd seen in *Self, Glamour, Vogue, Bazaar, Shape,* and other diet books. Then another thought hit me. *God, You made me; what should I weigh?*

I realized my perceptions were so warped that I would pick a weight far too light for my tall but petite frame. I got very quiet and listened again for the still, small voice. A figure floated into my head; I scribbled the number down and hid it in my Bible. It was more than my former anorexic one hundred three pounds. I initially thought one hundred ten pounds would be nice, but I wrote down another figure.

I got up from the floor, grabbed the scales, and climbed atop my bedroom chair to place them in the attic access in my bedroom closet. God had told me not to weigh myself. I would have to climb up there to get the scales, knowing all the while that I was deliberately disobeying God.

I went into my bathroom and splashed the tears from my face. I headed straight for the grocery store. I walked down the juice aisle, sensing so strongly that God was leading me to buy two quarts of unfiltered organic apple-strawberry juice and a couple gallons of purified water. I had never had unfiltered juice before. The next day would begin a new way of life for me. I was not fasting to lose weight; I was fasting to fellowship with God.

My focus during this fast was not weight loss. I sensed God's presence and leading in this action. I sensed that He was pleased with me for repenting and choosing to fast and draw closer to Him. For the next three days, I drank apple-strawberry juice, straight or diluted, along with purified water. God sustained me in this fast to which He had called me. I went for walks and talked with Him. I listened to praise and worship tapes and wept in His presence.

Then the fast of food was over. Now it was time for me to learn a new lifestyle. I would eat until I was satisfied—not until I was engorged. Because I had never known the difference before, praying before eating took on a whole new meaning for me. At mealtime I offered up my food with thanksgiving. I thanked God that food was not my enemy, nor was it my satisfaction. It would bring strength to my body, and in turn, I would worship God. Fear thoughts would try to attack me: *If you eat that food you'll get fat! Starve yourself.* Gluttony would try to entice me: *That tasted good; you need to eat more!*

I was determined not to eat because it tasted good, but to eat because I was feeding myself. I refused to be mastered by my passions any longer. Inwardly I would listen and know when I was satisfied. Then I would put my fork down, not eating another bite.

I was so excited that God was developing this sensitivity in me; I never wanted to disobey it. Even when my family and friends encouraged me to eat more, I would just say, "No, thank you; I am satisfied!"

I felt great! I would walk a mile each night and pray and talk to God. I would not run to burn calories; instead I just walked and talked to God. It brought rest to me. I knew I was losing weight, but I decided not to even notice it.

Three weeks had passed, and my wedding was just a few days away. I had no idea how much I weighed, nor was I even interested. I did need to know that my dress would fit, so I tried it on. Not only did it fit—it hung a little loose! I laughed with joy! I would be able to wear my dress!

My wedding was wonderful, and when I came home to change into my going-away outfit, God stopped me.

"Now you can weigh yourself."

I got the scales down and stepped on them. The needle teetered between one hundred ten and one hundred twenty pounds. I jumped off the scale and grabbed my Bible. Flipping through it, I found the small slip of paper with the scrawled number. I had forgotten the number I had written down four weeks earlier. I opened up the paper. One hundred sixteen pounds! I jumped back on the scales in disbelief; it was my exact weight! I knew that God had healed my body. He had formed me in my mother's womb...He could heal me.

No longer was I interested in pleasing everyone else; I wanted to please God. He tells us He knows what we need even before we ask. He assures us we are fearfully and wonderfully made. He does not measure us by the seen, but by the unseen. The following scripture took on a whole new meaning to me.

> Therefore I tell you, do not worry about your life, what you will eat or drink; or about your body, what you will wear. Is not life more important than food, and the body more important than clothes?
> —MATTHEW 6:25

Thinking about these things is a waste of time! Jesus admonishes us that worrying can't add even an inch to our stature. He called the addition of an inch a simple thing. He said if you can't change the small and simple, it is useless to worry about the big.

Fear and worry still tried to torment me

with negative thoughts: *What is going to happen when you have children? What if you can't lose the weight?* I fought back with the Word, not my own experiences. I would counter that God would perfect that which concerned me, and children were a blessing of the Lord. I refused to believe having children would destroy me physically.

I have four children, and though they periodically tax my strength and back, I have found God faithful for my figure. I relaxed, nursed, and enjoyed them without worrying about exercising back down to my prepregnancy size. With each one, I went back to my same size or smaller.

When you worry about your weight, your metabolism changes. It is a proven fact that fear and worry influence your digestive and metabolic system.

God has been faithful to keep me at that weight independent of diet and exercise. I have trusted Him to watch over my weight as long as I keep food in the proper place. I eat until I am satisfied. When I am home, I eat healthy because I want to take care of myself, not for weight loss. When it is time to celebrate, I enjoy food. But I eat to celebrate—not to celebrate eating.

Reordering the disorder of your weight and tumbling the food idol isn't about losing weight—it's about what you place your trust in. It's about how you spend your *self*. In this time I had humbled my *self* with fasting, and God had healed me.

Did you see your *self* in the last two chapters?
_____

Do you try to use food to meet needs only God can meet in your life? _____
_____

What are some of those needs?
_____
_____
_____
_____
_____
_____

Are they really being met, or are you still dissatisfied? _____
_____

Is food an idol in your life? _____
_____

Do you allow your weight to dictate your moods? _____

Do you feel good about your *self* when you are thin? _____

Do you feel bad about your *self* when your weight fluctuates? _____

What is controlling you?

_____

_____

_____

_____

_____

Father God,

Forgive me for allowing food and my weight to hold the wrong place in my life. I repent of idolatry. No longer will I measure my self by the scale. No longer will I count calories and diet. I will offer my food up with prayer and thanksgiving and trust You to show me when I have had enough. I will eat because You have provided food for my nourishment.

I will no longer be ruled by my stomach. I will no longer worry and fret over my weight. I will trust You. Heal my metabolism. I will no longer speak curses over my body; I will speak instead the truth of Your Word.

I will not abuse laxatives and diuretics. I will no longer purge my body by throwing up. Lord, rebalance and restore every area of my body. Since You formed me, show me what I should weigh and how I should eat. Speak it to me, and I will write it down. I turn this entire area of my life over to You. Take total control of it.

_____

Signature

_____

Date

Do not take it back. This is an area where you are not to take thought or measure your *self.* You have laid it aside.

Personal Notes

A DIET MAY CHANGE THE WAY
YOU LOOK, BUT A FAST WILL
CHANGE THE WAY YOU LIVE.
A DIET MAY CHANGE YOUR
APPEARANCE, BUT A FAST WILL
CHANGE THE WAY YOU SEE.

8

DIETING VS. FASTING

GOD TOLD ME *NOT TO DIET,* THEN HE TOLD ME *to fast.* This would seem a contradiction; both are a restriction of food. The difference lies in the purpose or motive that inspires them. A diet is designed to help you lose or gain weight. A change of diet may also be initiated to improve or correct health problems. Dieting is a natural physical application that alters our physical well-being, weight, or health. It changes the way we *look* or *feel.*

The fast I refer to is not for weight gain or loss. Nor is it limited to natural healing. It is not designed to change the way we look and feel but to change the way we *perceive* and *live*. *A diet may change the way you look, but a fast will change the way you live.* A diet may change your appearance, but a fast will change the way you see; it will alter your inner perspective. The world has perverted and reduced the fast, diminishing it to a diet. As such, it is not a spiritual renewal, but a physical one. Remember: The deepest transformations are wrought from the inside out.

Before my confrontation with truth, I'd only fasted to lose weight. Granted, I might have done a combination fast and diet, using reasoning such as this: *I need to lose weight, and I need direction, so I'll fast and accomplish both.* But on this type of fast, food and weight are still the focus. I have searched the Scriptures and found no reference in God's Word to a fast prescribed for weight loss. Your focus or motive on a fast will be your reward. If God isn't the center, it will be reduced to merely a time of denial.

The fast God led me to in the weeks prior to my wedding was not really about *food* at all—it was about *faith*. I previously placed my faith in my weight. During my fast I learned to transfer my dependency to God. I wanted to know Him; I wanted His truth in my innermost being. *I wanted transformation—not weight reduction.* Some of you do not need to lose weight, but you do need to break the tethers of its hold upon you. *You do not need to lose weight—you need to be loosed from weight!*

For too long you've measured your *self* by your bathroom scale, allowing it to dictate your moods and actions. You haven't been Spirit led—you've been weight led. I was weighed down by weight. My fast was not the turning point for my weight loss; it was the turning point of my faith. I had trusted in my *self,* only to be disappointed. I needed a spiritual and emotional overhaul. When I saw my idolatry:

> . . . I wept and chastened my soul with fasting.
>
> —PSALM 69:10, NKJV

David chastened his soul. It is your soul that rose up and gave weight preeminence. The soul confused slim with success. My soul longed for my father's approval and for the approval of men. My soul distorted my vision and perceptions until my physical size, shape, and weight dominated my thought life. I allowed my soul to lead me away from truth and moderation. My soul had to be chastened, and I had to be the one to do it. I had to rise up in the spirit and subject my soul to a chastening fast.

To *chasten* is to "discipline, purify, refine, clarify, and improve." Discipline is training, and

I had to be reprogrammed. Chastening was necessary to educate and cultivate a new me. This chastening by fasting began a purification and refinement of my soul and motives. This clarification brought insight so I could once again see clearly. Just as parents discipline their children to help them grow and learn right from wrong, my soul had to be chastened so it could improve and become wiser.

This refinement of my soul worked its way out and overtook my natural body and appetites. It was refined and purified by denial. Once the cravings of my soul were mastered, the cravings of my flesh followed. I was no longer enflamed with a passion for food. My body was denied salt and sugar and the use of these came back into balance.

When I could no longer comfort my *self* with food, I ran to God for comfort. I recovered all the lost thought-time and productivity that I had lent to my obsession with food and weight. All the hours of research and study were redirected. I had been relieved of the relentless burden of worry and fear over my weight. I felt the lightness of a captive set free from a hard and unforgiving taskmaster. My efforts were never good enough before, and I was never thin enough.

My emotions tipped back into balance. They were no longer tied to the fragile and fickle red arrow of my scale. Before, I hated my *self* when I was fat and loved my *self* when I was thin. My whole self-image could be shattered with the slightest changing of the indicator on my scale. The opinions or reactions of others to my physical shape dictated my sense of worth. Even when I was thin, I was tormented by the fear. The obsession caused me to live on the edge of extreme elation or deep depression. I was at the mercy of the scale and public opinion.

Fasting changed my perception by changing my focus. This in turn caused me to change the way I lived. I didn't live for food or weight— I lived for God. Even on a natural fast you will experience an increase in eyesight clarity. On a spiritual fast you will have your spiritual eyes stripped of scales that have blinded them.

After the fast I saw everything differently. My eyes were illuminated by God's Word and truth. My eyes shifted off me and onto my Father God. I could see the right path on which to walk, and I recognized my former errors in judgment. A fast will give you a new vision and a new direction for your life.

Like David, I had humbled my *self* with fasting (Ps. 35:13). When we humble our *selves* we bring our *selves* into submission or subjection. I brought my soul and, inevitably, my body under subjection to God's Word and truth. Before that I had been in submission to the cravings and appetites of my flesh and soul.

> I proclaimed a fast, so that we might
> humble ourselves before our God and
> ask him for a safe journey for us and
> our children, with all our possessions.
> —EZRA 8:21

Fasting positions us to acknowledge God's provision in our lives. It communicates that He is our source. We deny our *selves* food and tell Him, "I only want You and what You provide." I was embarking on a journey. I was changing seasons in my life. I was leaving the life of a single woman to join my life to my husband's. I was leaving my home state and stepping into the unknown. My future would bring children and travel. I wanted God's provision in every area of my life. Humbled by my inability, I called out for God's ability.

When we lay aside the daily routine of food, drink, pleasures, and leisure, we are able to reevaluate our priorities.

Fasting is not just about food; it is about separation. This separation represents a consecration to the Lord. A change in our relationship with Him. God posed this question to Israel:

> Is this the kind of fast I have chosen,
> only a day for a man to humble himself?
> Is it only for bowing one's head like a
> reed
> and for lying on sackcloth and ashes?

Is that what you call a fast,
>a day acceptable to the LORD?
>>—ISAIAH 58:5

The Israelites' fast had been reduced to religious motions and the denial of food. God was saying that they had reduced it to a one-day happening; they had lost the substance behind the fast. They had lost contact with God's heart on the matter. God imparts His outlook on this matter by outlining the fast that pleases Him:

Is not this the kind of fasting I have chosen:
to *loose* the *chains* of injustice
>and *untie* the *cords* of the yoke,
to *set* the oppressed *free*
>and *break every yoke?*
Is it not to *share* your food with the
>*hungry*
>and to *provide* the poor wanderer with
>*shelter*—
when you see the *naked,* to *clothe* him,
>and *not to turn away* from your *own*
>*flesh and blood?*
>>—ISAIAH 58:6–7, EMPHASIS ADDED

The fast God chooses loosens chains, unties cords, sets free, breaks every yoke, puts you in a position to share and provide for others, and turns your heart toward the needs of your own flesh and blood. God did not want a single day set aside occasionally to honor Him. He wanted a radical and profound change in lifestyle. Just as Jesus had confronted the Pharisees who tithed their garden herb yet neglected weightier things, so He addresses the issue of fasting. The Israelites were experts in the law but not in love. They turned from the poor and from doing good.

God told His people that if they would reach out beyond their *selves,* then everything they had tried to get for their *selves,* He would provide to them. We can dare to reach out beyond our *selves,* for He promises:

Then your *light* will break forth like the
dawn,
and your *healing* will quickly appear;
then your *righteousness* will go before
you,
and the *glory of the* LORD will be your
rear *guard.*
Then you will call, and the LORD will
answer;
you will cry for *help,* and he will say:
Here am I.
—58:8–9, EMPHASIS ADDED

God promises to bring His light to our darkness. To heal us and make us righteous. His glory will guard us, and He will answer our prayers and help us in our time of need. He repeats the outline of His conditions for this blessing, and He outlines His vision for their lives:

> If you *do away with* the yoke of *oppression,*
> with the *pointing finger* and *malicious talk,*
> and if you *spend yourselves* in behalf of the hungry
> and satisfy the needs of the oppressed...
> —58:9–10, EMPHASIS ADDED

God wants us to do away with the yoke of oppression. Eating disorders are a yoke of oppression—to those who bear it and to those around them. Oppressed people often oppress others. The pointing of the finger represents accusation and judgment of others. This usually involves comparisons, and if we are honest, we must admit to jealousy. God is admonishing us to get our eyes off our *selves,* to stop comparing and contrasting our *selves* with others whether we feel superior or inferior in comparison.

For too long we have spent all our time and energy on the needs of our *selves.* God wants us to spend our *selves* on the needs of others, to lift those who are oppressed. He wants the fast to be a turning point where we lay aside accusation and judging. He wants gossip and the destruction of slander stopped. He wants our focus to shift permanently from our *selves* to others. This means a departure from the realm of *self* consciousness, to an existence free from *self*ish motives, thus grasping God's heart. Then He reaffirms His promises:

> Then your light will rise in the darkness,
>> and your night will become like the noonday.
>
> The LORD will guide you always;
>> he will satisfy your needs in a sun-scorched land
>> and will strengthen your frame.
>
> You will be like a well-watered garden,
>> like a spring whose waters never fail.
>
> —58:10–11

Light will rise out of obscure darkness—so much light that your night will be as the noon day. Confusion will flee as you are assured of the promise of God's divine guidance. Your needs will be met, though all that surrounds you is scorched. Any hardship will only strengthen your frame. You will be like a well-watered garden, fed by a spring that never fails.

What more could you ask for?

But the list did not end there. Isaiah continues with God's promises:

Your people will rebuild the ancient ruins
   and will raise up the age-old founda-
      tions;
you will be called Repairer of Broken
   Walls,
   Restorer of Streets with Dwellings.

If you keep your feet from breaking the
   Sabbath
   and from doing as you please on my
      holy day,
if you call the Sabbath a delight
   and the LORD's holy day honorable,
and if you honor it by not going your own
   way
   and not doing as you please or speaking
      idle words,
then you will find your joy in the LORD,
   and I will cause you to ride on the
      heights of the land
   and to feast on the inheritance of your
      father Jacob.
The mouth of the LORD has spoken.

                 —58:12–14

None of the above benefits are the provision of the earth or the provision of man. They are the blessings of God. They are His blessings in response to a change of heart.

God is challenging us to fast so that we might become women who are transformed. Whenever Israel truly fasted and turned to

God for His assistance, He heard them. He responded with protection, provision, direction, and healing.

There is not one of us who in our own strength could provide all this. No matter how much money or wisdom we have, it will always fail us if we trust in it. God will never fail those who trust in Him.

Personal Notes

_____

_____

_____

_____

_____

_____

_____

_____

_____

_____

_____

_____

_____

_____

_____

_____

_____

JESUS WANTED THE WORD
OF GOD MORE THAN
NECESSARY BREAD.
HE DENIED HIMSELF THE
IMMEDIATE AND WAITED
UPON THE ETERNAL.

9

GOD'S FAST

G OD SHARES INSIGHTS AND SECRETS WITH THOSE who fear Him. The Book of Psalms talks about God's secrets.

> The secret of the LORD is with them that fear him; and he will shew them his covenant.
> —PSALM 25:14, KJV

The Bible tells us the story of a widow woman named Anna, who was very old. She holds a very important historical significance:

> She never left the temple but worshiped
> night and day, fasting and praying.
> Coming up to them [Joseph, Mary, and
> baby Jesus] at that very moment, she
> gave thanks to God and spoke about
> the child to all who were looking for-
> ward to the redemption of Jerusalem.
> —Luke 2:37–38

This very old woman who prayed and fasted could see better than the priest and the young people around her. She recognized Jesus as the long-awaited Messiah when He was only eight days old. The Pharisees couldn't even recognize Him at thirty-three, when He was casting out devils. Yet this elderly mother of the faith knew Him as He lay cradled in His mother's arms.

She was a true prophetess who encouraged those who were watching and waiting for Israel's redemption. Her prayers and fasting gave her prophetic insight.

You may or may not be a position to fast food. *But everyone is in a position to fast something.* It may be TV, telephone, maga-zines, sports, shopping, or hobbies. All of us have areas in which we hide our *selves* or waste time.

I challenge you to go before our Father and ask Him, by the power of the Holy Spirit, to expose any areas that could be fasted.

Every believer should fast periodically. It is

an act of separation to our Father. Some of you may be anorexic or bulimic. You need to fast all the images that have driven you to such abuse. Jesus gave us invaluable insight on fasting:

> Moreover, when you fast, do not be like the hypocrites, with a sad countenance. For they disfigure their faces that they may appear to men to be fasting. Assuredly, I say to you, they have their reward.
> —MATTHEW 6:16, NKJV

The one who fasts must do so with the right motivation. Jesus often berated the Pharisees for their religious, pious fastings done only for the attention it brought to them. Matthew 6:16 advises us to not be like the hypocrites.

Hypocrite is another name for impostor. An *impostor* is one who deceives others by the assumed character or false pretenses. The Pharisees pretended to fast unto the Lord when it was really done for the accolades of man. Their focus was their pious religious appearance, and their reward was the awe of man. They wanted to be great among men. But they received nothing from God's hand. You must choose between the reward of man or the reward of God. The religious fast is rewarded by man, while the broken and contrite are rewarded by God. Jesus continued:

> But you, when you fast, anoint your
> head and wash your face, so that you
> do not appear to men to be fasting, but
> to your Father who is in the secret
> place; and your Father who sees in
> secret will reward you openly.
>
> —Matthew 6:17–18, NKJV

If we are not hungry for God, it is because we have allowed our souls to be satisfied or satiated with other things. One morning when I was praying, I sensed the need for more of a hunger for God. I asked God to impart this hunger in me. At the time, I was recording my prayers in my journal; I waited for a response from God.

As fast as I could write, He answered me. He showed me I was the one responsible for my hunger level. He told me that if I wasn't hungry, it was because I was already full. Filled with the cares of this world. Filled with the pleasures and distractions of this world. He said that if I wanted to hunger in the midst of the abundance of things, I would need to fast. Fast the things that would distract, comfort, or distress me.

I was nursing my fourth son at the time, and I knew God was not calling me to fast food. He was calling me to fast other things that pulled me from His presence. I fasted TV, magazines, telephone calls that were not business related, and desserts. I rearranged my schedule to accommodate prayer and Bible reading.

I did this for about a month, and when the month was over, I had lost my appetite for many of the things I'd laid aside. I sensed an increased discernment. I had previously been desensitized by the abundance of noise, voices, and distractions. Now it was easier to hear God's voice.

The natural noise level in my house (with four young boys) had not varied; it was the static and noise in my mind that quieted. You may even now be saying, "Sounds great; but who has the time?" If we reserve fasting only for the times when we can physically leave or lock ourselves away, we will not fast.

As a mother, I am in a season where my children have legitimate demands on my time. God didn't tell me to check into a hotel room. He probably knew I would pass out and sleep the whole time. He wanted me to develop the ability to fast within my home and lifestyle.

God wants to be an integral part of our life every day, not just when we are on the mountain spiritually. I have had to develop a listening ear. One that can hear amid the din and noise of a full household. I have learned to listen while I take a shower, do dishes, and sort laundry.

This may shock you, but most of the time on my knees has been spent emptying my heart and repenting. Once this is done, I can usually hear God's voice whenever He desires to speak to me. When I prepare for a service, I study and make pages of notes. Often I never use them. I do the notes for my sake. To put my mind at ease. The real preparation for the service comes when I confess and cleanse my heart before the Lord.

This time of cleansing allows the Holy Spirit to flow through me. It separates the precious and holy (God's Word and anointing) from the vile (my agenda or prejudice). I separate my *self* for whatever time it takes until I sense this separation has taken place.

Fasting brings many benefits into our lives. Here are a few of the benefits:

1. Fasting creates a new hunger.

So we fasted and petitioned our God about this, and he answered our prayer.
—Ezra 8:32

When you fast . . . you become hungry. At first it may be hunger for food or whatever you are fasting, but as the initial hunger pangs or longings cease, a new desire or hunger is formed. Fasting causes you to hunger in the midst of abundance.

2. Fasting increases sensitivity to God.

> There was also a prophetess, Anna...She
> never left the temple but worshiped night
> and day, fasting and praying. Coming up
> to them at that very moment, she gave
> thanks to God and spoke about the child
> to all who were looking forward to the
> redemption of Jerusalem.
>
> —LUKE 2:36–38

From this account of the widow woman
Anna, we can see that fasting and prayer had
developed such a keen sensitivity in her that
she perceived the Christ child at a few days old.
She could hear clearly what God was saying.

I have found myself more sensitive after a
period of fasting. Our family decided to fast
television for a month. During this time we
spent time together playing, talking, and
praying. It puts us in closer touch with each
other, and consequently we became more sensitive toward our children's needs, fears, and
hopes. When the television was turned back
on, the difference was evident. What disturbed
me before now grieved me. Each of us viewed
violence as a personal violation. Our insight
had been honed when the constant barrage of
conflicting images was removed. Previously,
we had not been watching anything so horrible—it was just that the normal became so
violating after a time of separation.

3. Fasting works humility.

> Yet when they were ill, I put on sack-
> cloth and humbled myself with fasting.
> When my prayers returned to me unan-
> swered...
>   —Psalm 35:13

When we fast, we deny ourselves that which might satisfy us. When we deny ourselves food, we often feel our natural strength waning. In our weakness we find ourselves more dependent. It is a confrontation with the flesh, a time when we deny it satisfaction and provision. It is a time of turning aside from what we can provide and turning toward what God alone can give. This is often the setting for a confrontation between the spirit and the flesh. I personally find out just how strong a hold my flesh has on me when I fast. This revelation alone is humbling, but in order for the fast to be successful you must allow it to work humility in you. This replaces and reorders your perspective.

After forty days in the wilderness, Jesus was hungry physically. Satan came to tempt Him to use His position as the Son of God to create bread from stone. But instead Jesus humbled Himself and answered:

> It is written: "Man does not live on
> bread alone, but on every word that

comes from the mouth of God."
—MATTHEW 4:4

He wanted the Word of God more than necessary bread. He chose living bread over baked bread, and He became the Bread of Life. He denied Himself the immediate and waited upon the eternal.

4. Fasting chastens or disciplines.

> When I wept and chastened my soul with fasting, that became my reproach.
> —PSALM 69:10, NKJV

We have already discussed this benefit, but let's look at it again from another angle. When my children are disobedient or irresponsible with a toy, person, or privilege, we take it from them until it is once again in the proper perspective. In some instances, grounding could be viewed as a fast—a fast of privileges, friends, or sports. After they are returned, there is a new appreciation.

5. Fasting changes our appetite.

> While they were worshiping the Lord and fasting, the Holy Spirit said, "Set apart for me Barnabas and Saul for the work to which I have called them."
> —ACTS 13:2

If you've developed an appetite for something, you can crave it as long as you are eating it. For example, I am a fan of dark chocolate. Only dark chocolate appeals to me. If you were to offer me milk chocolate, I would not even want it. At a certain time each month I feel a sudden and strong urge for this pure dark chocolate. I crave it; when I have had it, I am fine for another month.

One time I was given a large supply of dark chocolate; I could have a piece each day if I wanted it. It wasn't long before I found myself *needing* my *daily* piece. Soon my supply was exhausted. For a few days I found myself returning to the pantry, hoping to find just one more piece somewhere. If I found a piece, then the cravings were gone. I had become accustomed to daily chocolate. When I was forced by lack of supply to fast from it, then I no longer hungered for it.

A fast is a break in our daily routine. It overcomes past cravings and restores or renews a fresh and new appetite. Whenever I come off a fast, I am hungry for healthy food. I am hungry for something new and fresh in my personal life as well. I want to leave behind the old and embrace the new.

6. Fasting increases our capacity.

> Go, gather together all the Jews who are in Susa, and fast for me. Do not eat

> or drink for three days, night or day. I
> and my maids will fast as you do. When
> this is done, I will go to the king, even
> though it is against the law. And if I
> perish, I perish.
>
> —ESTHER 4:16

This fast prepared Esther to overcome the fear of man—and even greater, her fear of death. This fast increased her capacity for self-sacrifice while it imparted wisdom. The survival of a nation depended on her willingness to lay down her life. She knew it was more than she could face in her present condition with her present information, so she drew on God's strength.

God told me, "If you want more than what you've seen, you'll need to be more than you've been."[1] Fasting positions you for just such an increase.

7. Fasting brings answers to prayer.

> Then you will call, and the LORD will
> answer; you will cry for help, and he
> will say: Here am I. If you do away with
> the yoke of oppression, with the
> pointing finger and malicious talk...
>
> —ISAIAH 58:9

A godly fast will bring answered prayer. It is the atmosphere for answers to questions, direction, help, and the revelation of God. It is a time when He says, "Here I am . . . I'm over here. Come to Me." This revelation may come through His Word, or as a still, small voice, or by a strong confirmation of what He has previously shown us.

8. Fasting leads to quick healing.

> Then your light will break forth like the dawn, and your healing will quickly appear.
>
> —Isaiah 58:8

God set up the fast as a manner of healing His people, a time when the darkness of oppression, depression, or infirmity is dispelled by light such as the dawn. When this light breaks forth, then healing soon follows. This could mean many things. It could be a revelation of sin, which, when repented of, allows healing to spring forth. It could mean a revelation of His will or Word that brings healing and freedom where there had been darkness or ignorance. This healing could be physical, mental, or spiritual.

Even natural medicine supports this. Many illnesses occur in the digestive system. A short fast gives your body a chance to refocus its energies on *healing* instead of on *eating*. (Please contact a physician before undertaking a fast if you are ill.)

9. Fasting opens the door to God's protection and provision.

Then your righteousness will go before you, and the glory of the LORD will be your rear guard.
—ISAIAH 58:8

God promised to be a guard before us and after us. A fast renews your righteousness and sends it on before you. Then as you give God the glory, He returns righteousness as your rear guard.

10. Fasting looses chains of injustice.

Is not this the kind of fasting I have chosen: to loose the chains of injustice and untie the cords of the yoke...
—ISAIAH 58:6

The kind of fast God leads us into has the power to loose any unjust chains that bind us. It also unties the cords tethering us to any yoke. But this application is not limited merely to a personal liberation for us—it represents God's desire to see us reach out and untie the ties that bind others and remove the chains of oppression.

11. Fasting frees the oppressed and breaks every yoke.

> Is not this the kind of fasting I have chosen...to set the oppressed free and break every yoke?
>
> —Isaiah 58:6

A fast is a time when we take our eyes off our *selves* and our needs and look around at the oppression and pain of others. In response we learn to reach out in compassion and help, becoming agents of healing.

Jesus said that His burden was easy and His yoke was light. When we are carrying a burden other than His, it is cumbersome, awkward, and heavy. There is nothing more frustrating than feeling responsible for something over which you have no authority. It will weigh you down with hopelessness and frustration.

During a fast, God checks these areas in our lives and exposes the yokes of fear, worry, stress, and turmoil. He removes them and readjusts His yoke for our life, the one that keeps us dependent upon Him. If you are feeling weighed down, perhaps you are carrying too much.

12. Fasting motivates us to provide food for the needy.

> Is it not to share your food with the hungry...
>
> —Isaiah 58:7

The benefit is kind of obvious—if you are not eating because of a fast, then you are free to share your portion with those less fortunate. Maybe you should give away any food lingering in your refrigerator or pantry that has a significant pull on you. (I personally am never tempted by a can of beans, but chocolate is another story!) Share with someone else, but don't proclaim or herald your fast...just give to them. I used to find it very hard to keep my fasting a secret because I felt I had to give a reason or justification for everything I did. It is all right to just say, "No, thank you, not today; I have other plans," to a lunch or dinner invitation. We do not need to explain further.

Fasting is not a burden but a privilege. It is intimate and private. It originated in the secret place between you and God. He waits in the secret place for you to join Him. After we visit with Him in secret, He will reward us openly. *Inward transformation brings about outward anointing, blessing, and provision.* Inward transformation positions us for the promotion of the Lord. He will:

> Prepare a table before me
> in the presence of my enemies.
> You anoint my head with oil;
> my cup overflows.
> Surely goodness and love will follow me
> all the days of my life,

and I will dwell in the house of the Lord
forever.
—Psalm 23:5–6

This passage describes the open reward of
the Lord. It is a feast of provision; it brings an
assurance of His presence. Even in the midst
of opposition, the believer who fasts as an act
of separation from the world and unto God
receives the rewards of God.

In the past, how have you viewed fasting?

_____

_____

_____

Have you been prone to diet? _____

_____

Have you ever fasted to show your desire for
a turning point or answers? _____

_____

_____

As you read the two chapters on fasting, did
you feel a desire stirring in you to fast?

_____

_____

If you did, I believe it is the Holy Spirit calling

you to a deeper level in your walk with God. Separate your *self* to Him.

Ask God to reveal the influences and areas that stand as hindrances between you and a deeper relationship with Him. Be still, listen, and then list the areas He reveals:

_____

_____

_____

_____

_____

_____

How can you pull away from these hindrances?

_____

_____

_____

_____

_____

Personal Notes

PERSONAL NOTES

WE HAVE NOT ALLOWED
THE IMAGE OF CHRIST
TO BE IMPRINTED UPON US
AS DEEPLY AS THE IMAGE
OF THE WORLD.

10

TEARING DOWN IDOLS AND BUILDING ALTARS

SINCE ISRAEL IS A NATURAL EXAMPLE OF OUR spiritual walk with God, we can look at the strengths and weaknesses of the Israelites and learn from them. Whenever one of the kings of Israel or Judah set his heart to serve God and walk in His righteous commands, God would hear the people's prayers and restore and deliver them from their enemies. But often the very next generation found themselves right back in idolatry. They'd witnessed firsthand the miraculous deliverance of God whenever they returned to Him; they knew

His mighty works and power; they knew His righteous judgment on their sin and unbelief...yet it would seem they were bent on repeating the idolatry of their fathers. It was a cycle that repeated itself again and again. Why? Because though there had been repentance, the presence of idols remained in their land. King Jehoshaphat is an example of this:

> In everything he walked in the ways of his father Asa and did not stray from them; he did what was right in the eyes of the LORD. *The high places, however, were not removed, and the people continued to offer sacrifices and burn incense there.* Jehoshaphat was also at peace with the king of Israel.
>   —1 KINGS 22:43–44, EMPHASIS ADDED

Though Jehoshaphat did not stray, he did not pave a way for others. He did not clear a path for his people or the son who would follow him. So the people continued in their idolatry. With the high places intact, the spirit of idolatry never left. It remained before the eyes of the people. Jehoshaphat was also at peace with the king of Israel—a peace forged through compromise. During his reign, the kings of Israel were wicked. Ahab was the first, followed by his wicked son Ahaziah, who inquired of Baal-zebub!

It was not up to the people to tear down

these high places—it was for the king to do.
His eyes were enlightened. He knew the difference between the truth and a lie. He
clearly saw the spiritual forces of wickedness
and the power of God. He possessed the
authority and power necessary to pull them
down, but alas he did not.

For the sake of a righteous king, Israel was
delivered from enemy attacks from without.
But inside the kingdom a war waged on the
battleground of compromise—one fought by
the righteousness remnant and their enemy,
the wicked majority. Israel's spiritual bondage
remained intact. The blind cannot safely lead
the blind; only those with sight can lead.

> Leave them; they are blind guides. If a
> blind man leads a blind man, both will
> fall into a pit.
>
> —Matthew 15:14

It is the responsibility of those who see to
direct. Hezekiah was a king with foresight.
Here is the description of his spiritual reign
over Judah:

> He did what was right in the eyes of the
> LORD, just as his *father David* had done.
> *He removed the high places,* smashed the
> sacred stones and cut down the Asherah
> poles. He broke into pieces the bronze
> snake Moses had made, for up to that

time the Israelites had been burning
incense to it. (It was called Nehushtan.)
—2 Kings 18:3–4, emphasis added

How interesting. Hezekiah was not as direct
a descendant of David as Jehoshaphat—he
was even further removed. Yet Hezekiah
earned this distinction because he served God
with all his heart just as David had done.
Therefore God awarded him David's lineage.
Jehoshaphat received the heritage of his natural father, Asa, while Hezekiah received the
heritage of his spiritual father, David. Hezekiah
was valiant for the Lord. He tore down the
idols of the people, even the one serpent
Moses had fashioned. He recognized people
had idolized even what God had done. I'm
sure he was not necessarily popular with the
people for his position, but he was popular
with God.

Hezekiah trusted in the Lord, the God
of Israel. There was no one like him
among all the kings of Judah, either
before him or after him. He held fast to
the Lord and did not cease to follow
him; he kept the commands the Lord
had given Moses. *And the Lord was with
him;* he was successful in whatever he
undertook. He rebelled against the king
of Assyria and did not serve him.
—2 Kings 18:5–7, emphasis added

Not only did he do what was right, but he held fast to the Lord and never ceased to follow him. This set him apart and above all the kings of Judah. The highest honor given him—the one that distinguished him as a righteous king—was the fact that "the LORD was with him." God was alongside him, making sure any undertaking of his would be successful.

The second portion of this verse contrasts him again with Jehoshaphat. Hezekiah would not make peace with nor pay tribute to the king of Assyria. This king represented the height of evil and arrogance in his time just as Ahab did in his. Hezekiah refused to succumb to his threats and intimidation, even though he had destroyed every other nation that rebelled against him.

When we don't tear down the high places, we find ourselves again serving and paying tribute to idolatry. You may question, "Am I a leader? Am I not a mere woman? What could I do? How could I possibly tear down any high places?"

Have you not repented? Do you not have sight? Have you not been given authority, power, and position?

> ...Jesus Christ, the faithful witness, the firstborn from the dead, and the ruler over the kings of the earth. To Him who loved us and washed us from our sins

in His own blood, *and has made us kings and priests to His God* and Father, to Him be glory and dominion forever and ever. Amen.

—Revelation 1:5–6, NKJV,
EMPHASIS ADDED

Not only is a kingly anointing on your life, but there is also a priestly anointing. Now tear down the high places. Though you may not possess authority in a natural earthly kingdom, you do in the heavenlies. You have the delegated authority of the Son of God; you have His Word; you have been washed in His blood; and He has all glory and dominion forever!

You have been granted a view high above all this present deception and darkness. Your eyes have been enlightened by the Truth to the truth—and it has set you free. Refuse to pay homage, tribute, or honor to idols any longer. Stand strong and do not be entangled again with the yoke of slavery.

It is for freedom that Christ has set us free. Stand firm, then, and do not let yourselves be burdened again by a yoke of slavery.

—Galatians 5:1

Do you know you can be set free and then become encumbered again? You can be free in Christ and entangled again with the yoke of

religion. You can be free in Christ and entangled again with the world. You must uproot
those influences in your life. You must con-
front those hidden desires. It is sad, but the
desire of many in the church is to be *like*
the world, but not *part* of her. Listen to the
anguish of God when Israel longed for rela-
tions with this present world:

> ...I was crushed by their adulterous
> heart which has departed from Me, and
> by their eyes which play the harlot after
> their idols.
> —EZEKIEL 6:9, NKJV

Israel just looked with their eyes and
longed in their heart. Ezekiel did not say they
had actually committed idolatry yet. He knew,
for God saw beyond their words and actions
into the hidden realm of the heart, and there
He found adultery. They longed for an idol
god while they were in covenant with the one
true God. The problem: We have not allowed
the image of Christ to be imprinted upon us
deeper than the image of the world has been
imprinted upon us

How different are we today? Do not many
of us long to look like the daughters of the
world? If we could just have their image—and
God too! You stand at this moment surrounded by the light of truth. The things I
bring before you I will bring to you in the

presence of this light. It is not my objective to be judgmental or critical, though what I say might sound so at first. Please hear it in light of the truth, because the lie has permeated the church for far too long.

I am not addressing the *lost in the world* but the *confused in the church*. Why are so many Christian women conforming to the image of this world? Why do we consult their periodicals on how to dress, how to wear our makeup, and how to find a man? Why do we watch hours of their adulterous and seductive entertainment at movies and on TV?

Recently I was horrified as I listened to one pastor share his disappointment and shock over a conversation he had with another pastor. This pastor of a large church had bragged to him that he'd spent over fifty thousand dollars on plastic surgery for his wife. He shared how in surgery she'd had it "put in," "sucked out," "redone," and now looked like a famous actress. He noticed this pastor wasn't impressed, so he justified his position. "Her job as a pastor's wife is to stay pretty so I won't be tempted." (Since when do sexually attractive women cure men of lust?)

"How used she must have felt!" I commented.

He shook his head, adding that she didn't care; she liked it, and she wanted to look good.

Another precious woman wrote to share

how her father, a pastor, suggested she have breast implants so "she could catch a husband." He offered to pay for the surgery, explaining that she was presently "a nine," but this would make her "a ten." She *did* want a husband, and her father *would certainly only want the best for her*...so she did it.

Now years later she is married, and her husband couldn't care less about her breast size. But the implants have become capsulated and need to be removed. There is some fear that silicone could be leaking into her body. She was not able to nurse her children, and she wishes she'd never had implants. The surgery to remove them will be very costly and will leave her scarred. She urged me to share her testimony to warn others.

Not long ago I received a ministry newsletter with an appeal for funds. It seemed the wife was in desperate need of surgery, and the couple did not have insurance.

I prayed, "God, do you want our ministry to send money?"

The answer came immediately. "Send no money! She is having cosmetic surgery."

I was shocked, and my hand shook as I held the letter. I read it again. Nothing in the wording implied cosmetic surgery. In fact, they made it sound like a matter of life and death. Surely I hadn't heard right. Later I inquired, and I found out that I had indeed heard correctly. They used the anointing on their ministry and played on the sympathy of God's people to deceptively raise funds.

Am I saying all cosmetic surgery is wrong and those who have it are going to hell? No. *I am questioning the motive.* What represents sin for one person may not be sin for another. I am asking, "To what image are you conforming?"

We know what image the world is serving, but what image is the church serving? Do sexually attractive woman prevent lust? Or do they fan the wrong fire? Are we believers or not? Is the cross powerless to destroy lust? Are Christian women to aspire to be like the world in order to win the world's acceptance? Does acceptance by the world bring the lost into the kingdom?

I believe the Book of James gives us a definite answer:

> Adulterers and adulteresses! Do you not know that friendship with the world is enmity with God? Whoever therefore wants to be a friend of the world makes himself an enemy of God. Or do you think that the Scripture says in vain, "The Spirit who dwells in us yearns jealously"?
> —James 4:4–5, NKJV

The New International Version reads, "Friendship with the world is hatred toward God." How much clearer do you need it? An adulteress has a covenant with one while involved mentally or physically with another. For too long our goal has been to become like the world so they could embrace us. No! They are not to embrace us. They are to embrace Christ. We are to live in such a way that *He* is lifted up (John 12:32). We are called to declare truth in the midst of a lost and dying world. Peter warned the believers of his day this way:

> Dear friends, I urge you, as aliens and strangers in the world, to abstain from sinful desires, which war against your soul.
>
> —1 PETER 2:11

Do aliens and strangers *conform* or *stand out?* The world understands why they need outward transformation: This present life is all they live for. They drape themselves outwardly to hide their inward emptiness. But it confuses them when Christians who have supposedly experienced inward transformation major on the outward. They look at us as if to question, "I know why I need to look this way...I am empty inside. Why do you need what I have already found to be empty?" We are to tell them of our world, not long to fit in with theirs. We are to come out and be separate, not blend.

The first part of declaring truth is to live it. I removed all the *Glamour, Vogue, Harper's*

Bazaar, Self, Fit, and *Victoria's Secret* catalogs from my house. After all, did I really want my sons to begin to think these were the types of women they should desire? Do you want your daughters turning to them for advice? I put their images away from me. I refused to buy their subscriptions or order their products.

We refused most of the cable channels and turned off the TV. This tuned out the seductive imagery, which, though it lasts but a second, imprints its image upon the canvas of my mind and the minds of those I love.

> Depart, depart, go out from there!
>> Touch no unclean thing!
> Come out from it and be pure,
>> you who carry the vessels of the LORD.
> —ISAIAH 52:11

This is also a New Testament command, not merely an ancient levitical law. Paul repeats it, and in this modern translation it is made very clear:

> And what union can there be between God's temple and idols? For we are the temple of the living God. As God said: "I will live in them and walk among them. I will be their God, and they will be my people. Therefore, come out from them and separate yourselves from them, says the Lord. Don't touch their

filthy things and I will welcome you."
—2 Corinthians 6:16–18, nlt

Do we want to be vessels that carry the precious? Then we must come out and be separate. This means purging our *selves* of the filthiness of the flesh and spirit so we can shine as a beacon and speak again the true words of God, words whose power is not diminished or contradicted by ungodly action or desires. We must tear down the spiritual darkness by the power of obedient lives.

If you return,
then I will bring you back;
You shall stand before Me;
If you take out the precious from the vile,
You shall be as My mouth.
Let them return to you,
But you *must not* return to them.
—Jeremiah 15:19, nkjv, emphasis added

When we return to Him, He brings us back, and then we can stand before Him. When we separate the precious from the vile, the truth from the lie, He put His words in our mouth. Then God warns us, "Welcome them when they return to you, *but you must not return to them*. They can come to you on the terms of truth, but you are not to go to them on the ground of compromise."

Personal Notes

_____

_____

_____

_____

_____

_____

_____

_____

_____

_____

_____

_____

_____

_____

_____

_____

_____

_____

_____

_____

PERSONAL NOTES

In Christ our focus
is restored again
to the eternal.
By losing sight of
the *seen* we gain
the *unseen*.

11

IF I'M NOT WHAT I WEIGH...WHAT AM I?

W̲HO DEFINES A WOMAN? WHAT DEFINES HER? We already know we cannot trust the definition of our culture, since it defines women in terms of the physical. The goal of a fallen culture is to be sexually attractive because it is emblazoned with lust. (See Romans 1:26–27.)

Though it begins with apparent innocence, young girls become enmeshed in the fantasy of growing up to be beautiful and desirable. After all, nearly every childhood movie alleges that it is the young and beautiful who marry and find happiness. Yet we've grown up and discovered that attractiveness is not enough to hold a family together. This dream rings hollow in our culture, with more than half of all marriages ending in divorce.

When the world's fantasy of the perfect family didn't work, our culture re-created its image of the ideal woman, in turn redefining the family. Society encouraged women to leave behind their bondage of servitude. Women were urged to become the master of their own destiny. The new image claimed that motherhood is boring—why waste your time on children when you can have a career? Stay-at-home mothers were despised as weak and lazy; the image of the independent career woman was embraced. Why not have it all! As the image demoralized, love was replaced with lust—a lust for power, security, and control. The image of a desirable woman changed from the gentle, faithful, and maternal to that of a free-spirited, self-willed wantonness. From a nurturer to a controller.

Yet from the very beginning God created woman to support, to complete—not to compete. This is the case whether a woman is married or single. Woman are nurturers by nature, and this strength can be translated to the professional as well as personal. Whether a woman is a single doctor or a stay-at-home mother, she can still bring the nature of a servant to any level. Not simply because she is a woman but because she is a Christian. We have a genderless command to:

> Above all, love each other deeply,
> because love covers over a multitude of
> sins...Each one should use whatever
> gift he has received to serve others,
> faithfully administering God's grace in
> its various forms.
>
> —1 PETER 4:8–10

Independent of our marital, professional, or social status, our talents and abilities are not to be used to serve our *selves,* but to serve *others.* We each have an opportunity to serve God in our unique sphere of influence. God plants each of us in various soils to accomplish His purpose.

The world is preaching an opposing gospel. Almost without exception, the covers of secular women's magazines boast young, seductive women and promise to reveal the secrets to great sex, ageless beauty, and thinner thighs. All of these are meant to entice subscribers with *self* gratification. They offer slavery to the lust of this world while God offers servitude. Their message: Live for the moment, live for pleasure, live for your *self!*

But what is the message of Christ? How can those of us who know the truth help spread the truth?

Though most women would never say outright, "I am what I weigh," still that concept was believed and obeyed at some level. In doing so, we conformed to an image and to the lies propagated by those who fashioned or manufactured the concept. Our former actions and lifestyle validated it. Now that we have turned our backs on the lie, we need to find our purpose. Letting go of lies can be frightening until truth is revealed. In obedience we renounced the lie and its idolatry; now we need to glean the precious from the vile. Most of us were led astray because we were looking—no, longing—for someone to define us.

I remember my freshman year in college. I found myself with more options than direction. In high school, classes are scheduled to accomplish the goal of graduation and not to focus on any specific area of study. I'd run away out west, far from all that was familiar; then I lost my bearings. Removed from my usual frame of reference, I felt vulnerable and confused. I wanted to dream yet didn't dare fail.

I wanted to study premed. but I feared I wasn't smart enough. I'd scored high on the required ACT exam but only modestly on the SAT exam. I wasn't certain if I was smart, stupid, or somewhere in between. During the first semester I went to the university guidance counselor and shared my dilemma. I requested additional testing in order to determine first, if I was smart enough, and second, if I had the aptitude.

When test day came I was a nervous wreck. I felt as though my whole future hung in the balance. It was a week or so before the results would be available. When I returned for the interpretation of the results, I was disappointed. My aptitudes ranged from dean of women to a podiatrist. My IQ results were inconclusive as well. "You're creative and excel at math and science. You are smart enough to be whatever you choose," the guidance counselor assured me.

"Are you certain?" I questioned.

"Yes. As long as you apply yourself, you can do anything," she answered.

This was not what I wanted to hear. I wanted precise and specific direction in order to apply myself. I wanted her to say something like this: "These test results show without a doubt that you can be a doctor in this field of medicine."

I questioned her further. "But what if I *don't* apply myself? Will I still succeed?"

Of course this question was stupid, and I'm sure at that moment she questioned the test results herself, for she glanced again at the folder in her hand. With a perplexed look she assured me that if I did *not* apply myself I would *not* be successful. As I left I thought, *I am not smart enough. I will not even try if there is a chance I might fail. I will choose another area of study.*

What did I want from her? I wanted her to

define me. I wanted her to remove all the *self* doubt that clouded my mind. I wanted clear directions to eliminate all chances for failure. I wanted a guarantee. I wanted her to tell me who I was and what I could and could not do. By taking the test I wanted conclusive direction. When I did not get this, I floated through college aimlessly. I wanted the test to tell me what I myself doubted. I wanted her professional faith in me to overcome my insecurities and fears. I could believe in the test, I could believe in her, but I found it difficult to believe in my *self*.

I continued my search elsewhere. At that stage in my life I received a lot attention from guys—perhaps one of them would define me. I moved in and out of relationships trying to find a fit. I chose guys who were hard to please and tried to be whatever they saw in me. I was like a chameleon. If they wanted me to be intelligent, I pursued academics. If they found me attractive, I was seductive. But it was always just a matter of time before I grew discontented. As soon as they molded or labeled me, I became uncomfortable and broke off the relationship. I realized their perceptions were inaccurate because I was living a lie by pretending to be someone I was not.

I had been pretending for a long time. At first it had been easy. There was the pretend me and the real me. The projected image and the protected one. But it was not long before the distinctions began to blur. The projected me was so busy trying to win approval and give the appearance of strength that I soon forgot who I really was, who it was I was protecting. As this progressed, I didn't like being alone. I wanted to be in a constant social setting. If you couldn't show me a good time, I didn't want to be around you. I was shallow and thoughtless. I was nothing more than what you saw. I was what I weighed, what I wore, who I dated. Like so many, I'd conformed to the cultural image and felt empty and lost.

My own fear of failure and desire for approval from men drove me to live such a lie. I chose to allow those around me to define me. I conformed to a lie. I could blame my father, boyfriends, a painful past, or brazen cultural influences, but the truth is, I had been void of truth, so I embraced lies.

Until I met Jesus, *the Truth* was not in me. I had to spurn the man-made information to embrace transformation. Transformation could only come by renewing my mind, by reading His Word. This meant I had to leave behind my former ways.

Many of you were already acquainted with Jesus when you began this book. But in this area of image, you were more acquainted with the message of the world than the message of Christ. I believe as you have read you've recognized and repented of these sympathies. This has released and empowered you to walk in truth. It is my prayer that you would never be entangled again. You've been untethered from the lie; now I want you bound to truth.

Jesus is that truth. As we live and apply His truth, we will walk on the path of ever increasing light.

> The path of the righteous is like the first gleam of dawn, shining ever brighter till the full light of day.
>
> —Proverbs 4:18

The prayers and steps you've taken in good faith have placed your feet on the path of righteousness. At the first gleam of dawn, the light is dim, but as we continue toward the light of His Word it grows brighter. The psalmist said, "Thy word is a lamp unto my feet, and a light unto my path" (Ps. 119:105, KJV). Our understanding is illuminated as we read His Word. It is important to approach the Word with humility. There is danger when we go to the Word to gather information to establish our opinions or beliefs. We then read what we believe, instead of believe what we read. When we go to the Word with a teachable, meek, and humble heart we are transformed. Dim eyes are flooded with the light of spiritual wisdom and understanding for the revelation of God.

> I pray that your hearts will be flooded
> with light so that you can understand
> the wonderful future he has promised
> to those he called. I want you to realize
> what a rich and glorious inheritance he
> has given to his people.
> —EPHESIANS 1:18, NLT

In Christ is embodied every dream and
hope, not only in heaven but as an inheritance for us on earth. He gives us purpose,
plans, and a future. His death defines our life.

> *Set your minds on things above, not on*
> *earthly things. For you died, and your*
> *life is now hidden with Christ in God.*
> When Christ, who is your life, appears,
> then you also will appear with him in
> glory.
> —COLOSSIANS 3:2–4, EMPHASIS ADDED

He is our life. He is "Christ in you, the hope
of glory" (Col. 1:27). Because our lives are
hidden in Him, our mind, desires, and affec-
tions should be set on things above, not on
earthly things. When Adam and Eve were in
the garden, their minds went from the heavenly and eternal to the earthly and temporal.
In Christ our focus is restored again to the
eternal. By losing sight of the seen we gain
the unseen. At the revelation of God's glory
we will be seen for what we really are.

Paul continues his letter to explain this transformation:

> ...since you have put off the old man with his deeds, and have put on the new man who is renewed in knowledge according to the image of Him who created him.
>
> —Colossians 3:9–10, NKJV

At the time of our rebirth we put on a new man (or woman) who is being renewed or regenerated inwardly until it takes on the image of its Creator. We will be restored to the original image God intended for us. No longer will we be formed in the image of man; we are once again created in the image of God.

When I look at God's holiness, then look at myself, it seems impossible that I have been created in the image of God! *Looking at ourselves we see the possible; looking at God we see the impossible.* What is impossible with man is possible with God. We are not to measure what God can do with and through us by what we have done. We are not the focus; the possibility of our new image is not based on us—but on a victory Christ has already won. It does not matter how many times you may have tried and failed; it is not about you or your ability.

Do not be afraid; you will not suffer shame.
Do not fear disgrace; you will not be
humiliated.
You will forget the shame of your youth
and remember no more the reproach of
your widowhood.
—ISAIAH 54:4, EMPHASIS ADDED

This is God's promise. An invitation to leave behind our prison of fear. He assures us that shame and humiliation will not be our future, and He promises to erase all the shameful memories and reproach of our past. This promise is available to each child of God. It is for those who will dare to believe and thereby mix His precious words with faith. *Your past is not your future!* He holds out the hope of a future free from the fear of failure. In the Book of Philippians Paul shared his feelings of imperfection, and then he gave us the key to his walk with God:

Forgetting what is behind and straining toward what is ahead...
—PHILIPPIANS 3:13

When we look to our past we forsake our future. When the woman taken in adultery was brought before Jesus, He told her, "Go, and sin no more" (John 8:11, KJV). Notice He did not say, "I know you have a problem with men because you never had a healthy relationship with your father. I want you to go through six months of counseling, and once you have figured this all out then you will be able to go and sin no more." Her past did not matter; His forgiveness and word held the power to free her. *Looking again to the past arouses doubt and reawakens our self consciousness, thus reducing our God consciousness.*

You may say, "It is all too simple." Human nature is often drawn to the difficult and complex, but I find God most often in the pure and simple. You are free. The light has shone on your path. Now the choice is yours. Will you walk in the light?

Until God imparted His purpose and plan into my life, I felt entirely purposeless. Our purpose or calling defines us. He defined us with His death:

> You are a chosen people, a royal priesthood, a holy nation, a people belonging to God, that you may declare the praises of him who called you out of darkness into his wonderful light.
>
> —1 Peter 2:9

God defines us because He has chosen us. He separated us from the world to bring us back to Himself. He delivered us out darkness into the light so that we would declare His praises. We belong to Him, purchased by the priceless blood of His Son.

My computer screensaver scrolls this saying;

> Until you find something worth dying
> for…you're not really alive.

Do you know an estimated one thousand women will die this year for the sake of being thin? Thin is not something worth dying for. These women die because they have no real reason to live; they are not truly alive. Because Jesus thought you were something worth dying for, you can be truly alive. He exchanged His vibrant, abundant life for your gray and lifeless one.

By whose definition will you live?

PERSONAL NOTES

PERSONAL NOTES

_____

_____

_____

_____

_____

_____

_____

_____

_____

_____

_____

_____

_____

_____

_____

_____

_____

NOTES

CHAPTER 2
The Truth

1. James Strong, *Strong's Exhaustive Concordance* (Grand Rapids, MI: Baker Book House, 1979), s.v. "know."

CHAPTER 3
The Image of the Lie

1. Herbert Lockyer, *Nelson's Illustrated Bible Dictionary* (Nashville, TN: Thomas Nelson Publishers, 1986), s.v. "idol."

CHAPTER 9
God's Fast

1. Lisa Bevere, *Out of Control and Loving It!* (Lake Mary, FL: Creation House, 1996), 56.

BOOKS

OUT OF CONTROL AND LOVING IT!   LISA BEVERE

 In this exciting book, Lisa candidly shares how her life was a whirlwind of turmoil until she discovered that whenever she was in charge, things ended up in a mess. Witness her journey from fearful, frantic control to a haven of rest and peace under God's control.

This book teaches you how to surrender your life—your mate, children, finances, job, or ministry—to God. Are you holding on so tightly that God can't work in your life? Let go and discover the freedom and peace God intended you to have! Also available in audio.

177 pages ISBN 0-88419-436-1	Item #BKL001/$11.00

THE TRUE MEASURE OF A WOMAN   LISA BEVERE

 A woman often measures herself and her own worth according to the standards set by others around her. Her self-esteem rises and falls with the whims of popular opinion as she allows other people to control how she thinks about herself.

In her frank, yet gentle manner, Lisa exposes the subtle influences and blatant lies that hold many women captive. This is an interactive book designed with questions to help you unveil the truth of God's Word. These truths will displace any lies and also help you discover who you are in Christ. It is only then that you can stop comparing yourself to others and begin to see yourself as God sees you.

172 pages ISBN 0-88419-487-6	Item #BKL002/$11.00

Books (Cont'd.)

The Fear of the Lord   John Bevere

More than ever, there's something missing in our churches, our prayers, and in our personal lives. It's what builds intimacy in our relationship with God. It's what makes our lives real and pure. It's what transforms us into truly Spirit-led children of God. It is the fear of the Lord.

In this riveting book, John exposes our need to fear God. With his lovingly confrontational style, he challenges us to reverence God anew in our worship and daily lives. This profound message will provoke you to honor God in a way that will revolutionize your life. Also available in audio and video.

196 pages ISBN 0-88419-525-2	**Hardcover**
	Item # BKJ006/$15.00

196 pages ISBN 0-88419-486-8	**Softcover**
	Item #BKJ006S/$12.00

The Bait of Satan   John Bevere

Have you been trapped? This book exposes one of Satan's most deceptive snares used to pull believers out of God's will. It is the trap of offense. Jesus said, "It is impossible that offenses will not come" (Luke 17:1). The question is not, Will you encounter the bait of Satan? Rather, How will you respond? Don't let another's sin or mistake affect your relationship with God! Also available are a video and a thirty-day interactive study guide for group or individual study.

196 pages ISBN 0-88419-374-8	**Softcover**
	Item# BJK003/$11.00

90 pages ISBN 0-88419-447-7	**Study Guide**
	Item# SG01/$5.00

VIDEOS

ESCAPING ANGER   LISA BEVERE

Ask yourself:

- ❖ *Do you live on the edge of losing control?*
- ❖ *Has anger become a part of your personality?*
- ❖ *Do other people make you mad?*

You need to get free from anger. In this brutally honest video you'll hear truths that will set you free. This is an open and candid look at both the entanglement and the destructive force of anger. In this powerful teaching you'll discover:

- ❖ *The root of anger*
- ❖ *How to attack your problems, not people*
- ❖ *Taking responsibility*
- ❖ *How to lose a victim mentality*

Item # VCL002/$18.00

YOUR PAST IS NOT YOUR FUTURE   LISA BEVERE

Ask yourself:

- ❖ *Do you fight a constant cycle of defeat in your life?*
- ❖ *Do you feel as if you can only go just so far before an unseen chain snaps you back?*
- ❖ *Do you find yourself studying your past in order to protect your future?*

Break the cycle of fear and walk in the freedom that was purchased at so great a price. In the year of jubilee all past debts are forgiven, granting all in covenant a new beginning. It is your time to break free!

Item #VCL003/$18.00

OTHER AUDIO/VIDEO MESSAGES

by John and Lisa Bevere

VIDEOS

- *The Baptism of Fire*
- *Breaking Intimidation*
- *Does God Know You?*
- *Don't Faint Before Your Harvest*
- *Passion for His Presence*
- *Changed From Glory to Glory*
- *Cultivating a Pure Heart*
- *The Secret to God's Outpouring*
- *What Is Your Image of God?*
- *Led or Misled?*

AUDIOCASSETTE SERIES (3 TAPES)

- *Armed to Suffer*
- *By Order of the King*
- *Pursue the High Call*
- *Standing Strong in a World of Compromise*
- *Breaking Intimidation*
- *Walking With God*
- *Breaking Through the Resistance*

To order call: 1-800-648-1477 (U.S. only)
or 407-889-9617

To receive a free color catalog or JBM's free newsletter, *The Messenger,* or to inquire about inviting the ministry of John and Lisa Bevere to your organization, write to:

JOHN BEVERE MINISTRIES
P. O. Box 2002
Apopka, FL 32704-2002 U.S.A.
Tel: 407-889-9617
Fax: 407-889-2065
e-mail: jbm@johnbevere.org